Joyce Appleby on *Thomas Jefferson*
Louis Auchincloss on *Theodore Roosevelt*
Jean H. Baker on *James Buchanan*
H. W. Brands on *Woodrow Wilson*
Alan Brinkley on *John F. Kennedy*
Douglas Brinkley on *Gerald R. Ford*
Josiah Bunting III on *Ulysses S. Grant*
James MacGregor Burns and Susan Dunn on *George Washington*
Charles W. Calhoun on *Benjamin Harrison*
Gail Collins on *William Henry Harrison*
Robert Dallek on *Harry S. Truman*
John W. Dean on *Warren G. Harding*
John Patrick Diggins on *John Adams*
Elizabeth Drew on *Richard M. Nixon*
John S. D. Eisenhower on *Zachary Taylor*
Paul Finkelman on *Millard Fillmore*
Annette Gordon-Reed on *Andrew Johnson*
Henry F. Graff on *Grover Cleveland*
David Greenberg on *Calvin Coolidge*
Gary Hart on *James Monroe*
Michael F. Holt on *Franklin Pierce*
Roy Jenkins on *Franklin Delano Roosevelt*
Zachary Karabell on *Chester Alan Arthur*
Lewis H. Lapham on *William Howard Taft*
William E. Leuchtenburg on *Herbert Hoover*
James Mann on *George W. Bush*
Gary May on *John Tyler*
George McGovern on *Abraham Lincoln*
Timothy Naftali on *George H. W. Bush*
Charles Peters on *Lyndon B. Johnson*
Kevin Phillips on *William McKinley*
Robert V. Remini on *John Quincy Adams*
Ira Rutkow on *James A. Garfield*
John Seigenthaler on *James K. Polk*
Hans L. Trefousse on *Rutherford B. Hayes*
Tom Wicker on *Dwight D. Eisenhower*
Ted Widmer on *Martin Van Buren*
Sean Wilentz on *Andrew Jackson*
Garry Wills on *James Madison*
Julian E. Zelizer on *Jimmy Carter*

William Henry Harrison

Gail Collins

William Henry Harrison

THE AMERICAN PRESIDENTS

ARTHUR M. SCHLESINGER, JR., AND SEAN WILENTZ

GENERAL EDITORS

Times Books

HENRY HOLT AND COMPANY, NEW YORK

Times Books
Henry Holt and Company, LLC
Publishers since 1866
175 Fifth Avenue
New York, New York 10010
www.henryholt.com

Library of Congress Cataloging-in-Publication Data
Collins, Gail.
William Henry Harrison / Gail Collins.—1st ed.
p. cm.—(The American presidents)
Includes bibliographical references and index.
ISBN 978-0-8050-9118-2
1. Harrison, William Henry, 1773–1841.   2. United States—
Politics and government—1841–1845.   3. United States—History—
1783–1865.   4. Presidents—United States—Election—1840.
5. Presidents—United States—Biography.   6. Governors—Indiana—
Biography.   I. Title.
E392.C65 2012
973.5'8092—dc23
[B]   2011018976

Henry Holt books are available for special promotions and
premiums. For details contact: Director, Special Markets.

First Edition 2012

Printed in the United States of America
3   5   7   9   10   8   6   4

In memory of my father, Roy Gleason

Contents

Editor's Note

THE AMERICAN PRESIDENCY

The president is the central player in the American political order. That would seem to contradict the intentions of the Founding Fathers. Remembering the horrid example of the British monarchy, they invented a separation of powers in order, as Justice Brandeis later put it, "to preclude the exercise of arbitrary power." Accordingly, they divided the government into three allegedly equal and coordinate branches—the executive, the legislative, and the judiciary.

But a system based on the tripartite separation of powers has an inherent tendency toward inertia and stalemate. One of the three branches must take the initiative if the system is to move. The executive branch alone is structurally capable of taking that initiative. The Founders must have sensed this when they accepted Alexander Hamilton's proposition in the Seventieth Federalist that "energy in the executive is a leading character in the definition of good government." They thus envisaged a strong president—but within an equally strong system of constitutional accountability. (The term *imperial presidency* arose in the 1970s to describe the situation when the balance between power and accountability is upset in favor of the executive.)

The American system of self-government thus comes to focus in the presidency—"the vital place of action in the system," as Woodrow Wilson put it. Henry Adams, himself the great-grandson and grandson of presidents as well as the most brilliant of American historians, said that the American president "resembles the commander of a ship at sea. He must have a helm to grasp, a course to steer, a port to seek." The men in the White House (thus far only men, alas) in steering their chosen courses have shaped our destiny as a nation.

Biography offers an easy education in American history, rendering the past more human, more vivid, more intimate, more accessible, more connected to ourselves. Biography reminds us that presidents are not supermen. They are human beings too, worrying about decisions, attending to wives and children, juggling balls in the air, and putting on their pants one leg at a time. Indeed, as Emerson contended, "There is properly no history; only biography."

Presidents serve us as inspirations, and they also serve us as warnings. They provide bad examples as well as good. The nation, the Supreme Court has said, has "no right to expect that it will always have wise and humane rulers, sincerely attached to the principles of the Constitution. Wicked men, ambitious of power, with hatred of liberty and contempt of law, may fill the place once occupied by Washington and Lincoln."

The men in the White House express the ideals and the values, the frailties and the flaws, of the voters who send them there. It is altogether natural that we should want to know more about the virtues and the vices of the fellows we have elected to govern us. As we know more about them, we will know more about ourselves. The French political philosopher

Joseph de Maistre said, "Every nation has the government it deserves."

At the start of the twenty-first century, forty-two men have made it to the Oval Office. (George W. Bush is counted our forty-third president, because Grover Cleveland, who served nonconsecutive terms, is counted twice.) Of the parade of presidents, a dozen or so lead the polls periodically conducted by historians and political scientists. What makes a great president?

Great presidents possess, or are possessed by, a vision of an ideal America. Their passion, as they grasp the helm, is to set the ship of state on the right course toward the port they seek. Great presidents also have a deep psychic connection with the needs, anxieties, dreams of people. "I do not believe," said Wilson, "that any man can lead who does not act . . . under the impulse of a profound sympathy with those whom he leads—a sympathy which is insight—an insight which is of the heart rather than of the intellect."

"All of our great presidents," said Franklin D. Roosevelt, "were leaders of thought at a time when certain ideas in the life of the nation had to be clarified." So Washington incarnated the idea of federal union, Jefferson and Jackson the idea of democracy, Lincoln union and freedom, Cleveland rugged honesty. Theodore Roosevelt and Wilson, said FDR, were both "moral leaders, each in his own way and his own time, who used the presidency as a pulpit."

To succeed, presidents not only must have a port to seek but they must convince Congress and the electorate that it is a port worth seeking. Politics in a democracy is ultimately an educational process, an adventure in persuasion and consent. Every president stands in Theodore Roosevelt's bully pulpit.

The greatest presidents in the scholars' rankings, Washington, Lincoln, and Franklin Roosevelt, were leaders who confronted and overcame the republic's greatest crises. Crisis widens presidential opportunities for bold and imaginative action. But it does not guarantee presidential greatness. The crisis of secession did not spur Buchanan or the crisis of depression spur Hoover to creative leadership. Their inadequacies in the face of crisis allowed Lincoln and the second Roosevelt to show the difference individuals make to history. Still, even in the absence of first-order crisis, forceful and persuasive presidents—Jefferson, Jackson, James K. Polk, Theodore Roosevelt, Harry Truman, John F. Kennedy, Ronald Reagan, George W. Bush—are able to impose their own priorities on the country.

The diverse drama of the presidency offers a fascinating set of tales. Biographies of American presidents constitute a chronicle of wisdom and folly, nobility and pettiness, courage and cunning, forthrightness and deceit, quarrel and consensus. The turmoil perennially swirling around the White House illuminates the heart of the American democracy.

It is the aim of the American Presidents series to present the grand panorama of our chief executives in volumes compact enough for the busy reader, lucid enough for the student, authoritative enough for the scholar. Each volume offers a distillation of character and career. I hope that these lives will give readers some understanding of the pitfalls and potentialities of the presidency and also of the responsibilities of citizenship. Truman's famous sign—"The buck stops here"—tells only half the story. Citizens cannot escape the ultimate responsibility. It is in the voting booth, not on the presidential desk, that the buck finally stops.

—Arthur M. Schlesinger, Jr.

William Henry Harrison

Prologue

People sometimes ask me why I volunteered to write a biography of William Henry Harrison. Actually, it comes up quite a lot. Harrison's one-month term in office was really nothing more than a list of nonachievements (only president never to appoint a federal judge; his wife the only first lady since the construction of the White House who never saw it) and a cautionary tale about the importance of not making long speeches in the rain.

My answer is that I felt I owed him.

This goes back to a time when I was in Cincinnati, on a publicity tour for a book I'd written about gossip and its effect on politics in American history. Cincinnati is my hometown. It's also the place where Harrison settled, after a childhood in plantation Virginia and a stint governing the Indiana Territory. When I was in high school I won the local Veterans of Foreign Wars' "Speak for Democracy" contest and my reward was to read my speech to some of the veterans and my loyal parents at Harrison's tomb, which was large but rather bleak.

William Henry was a character in my gossip book—mainly to illustrate my theory that his embarrassment over having been criticized as too old and feeble to be president had led him to demonstrate his strength and virility by giving a nearly two-hour-long inauguration speech in bad weather, which made him sick and then—with the help of a team of overenergetic doctors—dead.

Since it is always a good idea to push the local angle, I was interviewed by an Ohio TV station while standing in front of a statue of Harrison, mounted on a steed I presumed was Whitey, the faithful companion he rode in the inauguration parade and which the ever-quotable John Quincy Adams dismissed as "a mean horse."

Later, visiting my family, I was telling the story of how Harrison was born a Virginia aristocrat but was marketed to the voters as a humble old soldier drinking cider in a log cabin.

"And he really had this big, beautiful house," I said, in what I thought was going to be the final word on the subject.

"Yes," my father said matter-of-factly. "That was a really big house."

Several seconds of silence.

"How do you know about William Henry Harrison's house?" I asked.

"I tore it down," he said somberly.

My father worked for the Cincinnati Gas and Electric Company, and he said that back in the 1960s he was told to get together a crew of workers and demolish the "Harrison Mansion," which was still standing on part of the site of the North Bend, Ohio, power station, where he worked.

I looked this up, my family's big intersection with presidential history. It turns out that the house was part of a Harrison family compound on two thousand acres of farmland that the Harrisons owned along the Ohio River. It was called The Point and was occupied by one of the Harrison sons, John Scott. William Henry's own sixteen-room home burned down before the Civil War. By then he was dead, as were nine of his ten children. His widow, Anna, moved into The Point with John Scott and his family, which included a Harrison grandson, Benjamin, who would eventually become president of the United States himself.

It was a serious landmark—home of one future president and proof of the lifestyle choices of his alleged log-cabin-dwelling grandfather. By the time the modern era came around, the two Presidents Harrison had become so blurred in history that the preservationists couldn't raise money to restore it. "The house now so desolate a picture, is of brick built in colonial style," a Cincinnati newspaper reported in 1940. "That hardware and glass in it, most of which is still intact, was brought over the Allegheny Mountains and down the river by boat . . . two features of unusual beauty are the circular staircase in the entrance hall and the original leaded glass transom over the front door."

Cincinnati Gas and Electric declared itself perfectly willing to hand over the house to any public-spirited group that wanted to move it someplace else, but the management was clearly a little worried that it would be declared a historic monument right there in the middle of the power plant. And one day they quietly ordered a crew of men, including my father, to decimate it.

So this book began as an act of familial penance.

Researching it, I was relieved to learn that there's another Harrison home that has been preserved—Grouseland, the house William Henry built for his family in Vincennes, Indiana, when he was sent there as territorial governor when he was still a young man in his twenties. It's a very impressive place even now, but back in 1801, when the territory had no roads and Vincennes had only about seven hundred people, it was regarded as the eighth wonder of the world. Everything had to be imported, often from Europe. Grouseland tells you more about Harrison than the North Bend home ever could have—how he wanted the people he was responsible for governing to see that, even though he was very young, he was a man to be reckoned with. How determined he was to make sure his children were raised at the same level of privilege that he had been on the Virginia plantation. Why Harrison, a man without any large personal fortune, was going to spend his entire life desperately searching for cash.

Besides catching pneumonia during his inauguration, Harrison is famous for things he didn't actually do. He didn't win a big military victory at Tippecanoe—it was a minor fight against an outnumbered village of Indians, and because Harrison screwed up the defense of his camp the white Americans suffered most of the casualties. He did better during the War of 1812. But his real impact on history arguably came from the work he did in the Grouseland years—acquiring several states' worth of territory from the Indians in deals that cost the federal government only pennies per acre. This is not a part of our history that we celebrate, and even back in 1840 the voters preferred the stories of battlefield heroics.

Politically, Harrison's greatest achievement was to star in what is still celebrated as one of the most ridiculous presidential campaigns in history. But even then, other men came up with the story line about Harrison the humble soldier and pushed it into the national memory forever with months of singing from *The Log Cabin Songbook* and dancing "The Log Cabin Two-Step."

William Henry's own contribution was to become the first presidential candidate to personally campaign for the job, and he willingly plowed into crowds to shake endless hands and at least pretend to remember all the veterans who wanted to reminisce about serving under him.

Then he won and then he died. I am going to take a big historic leap and guess that if he had lived—if Anna Harrison had accompanied her husband to Washington and demanded that he carry an umbrella at all times—William Henry would still not have been the sort of chief executive who gets his head carved on the side of a mountain. He was living in a bad time for presidents, that long gray period between Andrew Jackson and Abraham Lincoln when the great cloud of slavery and approaching civil war would make everybody—even an effective president like James Polk—seem like a historic asterisk.

There was nothing in Harrison's history that suggests transformational leader. If he had lived, the country would still have made its long march toward the Civil War. Perhaps the Whig Party would have made a bigger, longer impact if he had spent four years in the White House instead of John Tyler. But it is my experience that there are not many Americans, or even many American historians, who are particularly interested in speculating on what it would have meant if things had worked out better for the Whigs.

The William Henry Harrison story is less about issues than about the accidents of fate and silly campaigns. It's always tempting to look back on American history and marvel about how things were just like today. They weren't. In 1840, the nation was full of wide-open spaces, but it was also dark and dirty. In the countryside, people lived in small, gloomy homes. The cities were dangerous places full of violence, horse dung, and men who chewed tobacco and spit everywhere. Women could not vote, and the average baby had a life expectancy of about forty-five years.

Yet the campaign of 1840 seems so . . . modern. Besides

the cold pragmatism of the Tippecanoe mythmakers, what stuns us about the Harrison campaign is the apparent gullibility of the voters. The Whigs were describing him as a simple product of a log cabin in one breath and bragging about his father signing the Declaration of Independence in the next. Didn't they think the people were listening?

Well they were, in the same way we are today, although we can hear the rapid responses in less than a minute, while they had to wait a couple of weeks for the mail. The voters had their ears open for any suggestion that one of the candidates had an answer to their problems. And if not, they looked for the one who might have their trials in mind when he had to make a decision about banks or budgets or foreign affairs.

And William Henry Harrison answered the bill, sort of. He was very good at things paternal. As a general he was extremely kind to his men, willing to share their privations and the dangers to which he exposed them. He was open and friendly with people of every station. As a politician, his only consistent and passionate cause was getting federal aid for disabled veterans and for the families of those who had fallen. His own dinner table, which was crowded enough with his many relatives, was also filled with the widows and children of dead comrades.

His central mission was actually just taking care of his family. He had ten kids, plus quite a few orphan wards. If the land along the Ohio had produced enough money to support them all in a Virginia-gentry lifestyle, he probably would have spent his post-military life worrying about crops and livestock and going to the occasional testimonial dinner where his neighbors would recall the glories of the War of 1812. But as it was, he spent much of his time nagging important politicians to give him a job that would provide enough cash to bridge the difference between the farm's income and his household budget.

He reminds me in many ways of my own father, although unlike William Henry my dad really did come from humble roots. And unlike William Henry, his hard work did not pay off in the end with a sudden burst of fortune that would propel him into American history. But they both had to make their own way from the time they were young. They both found themselves responsible for a passel of kinfolk and they readily accepted the burden of providing for them.

If the Harrison mansion in Cincinnati had been preserved, school groups could go through it today, take note of the awesomeness of the architectural embellishments, and be tasked to compare the site to the vision of the log cabin homestead that the Whig Party marketed in 1840. It would be an excellent lesson in the unreliability of campaign literature, but my impression is that the youth of America is already cynical enough on this point.

Maybe someday he'll be repackaged in a way that's more inspiring—not as the guy who got elected president by pretending to be something he wasn't and then made a fatal inauguration speech in the rain, but as a struggling American dad in a difficult era, trying to keep food on the table and a roof over everybody's head. And maybe an imported leaded-glass transom over the door.

1

To the Manor Born

William Henry Harrison was born on February 9, 1773, seventh in a family of three boys and four girls, and in a way his destiny was determined by his birth order. The youngest sons of great families were at almost as much of a disadvantage in eighteenth-century America as they had been in medieval Europe. The oldest sons inherited the estate. Their parents could only hope their younger brothers would marry well, or at least stay out of sight and out of trouble—the modern concept of a career had not been invented yet. Control of the Harrison family plantation would go to the firstborn son, Benjamin. A life in law and then politics was mapped out for Carter, the second. When it came time to educate the third son, the Harrisons mainly seemed to be looking for a career that did not require expensive schooling.

The great hereditary name for a Harrison was Benjamin, and of course William Henry came too late for that as well. (When his grandson reached the White House in 1889, he was President Benjamin Harrison to the world, but Benjamin VIII on the family tree.) Benjamin I had arrived in this country in 1633, at the young colony of Jamestown, where he was

soon elected to the governing council. Future Benjamins
acquired and built up the family plantation, Berkeley, a vast
swath along the James River. Its grounds included the site of
what Virginians regarded as the first American Thanksgiving,
an event that was pretty much confined to prayer and lacked
the meal-oriented focus of the Massachusetts version.

Every generation of Harrisons included prominent office-
holders, but the greatest and most famous by far was William
Henry's father, Benjamin V—twice governor of Virginia and a
signer of the Declaration of Independence. He had become
head of the family suddenly, when he was nineteen and his
father was killed in a freak accident. (Going upstairs to close a
window during a thunderstorm, Benjamin IV was hit by a bolt
of lightning that also killed two daughters, who were nearby.)

Benjamin V, who the family reverently called The Signer,
was larger than life, standing six feet, four inches and quickly
going to fat. (John Adams, who had an on-again, off-again
friendship with him, called Benjamin "Jack Falstaff" after the
corpulent Shakespearean character.) Stories about The Signer
abounded. During the Second Continental Congress, when
there was a quarrel over who would assume the chairman's role,
Harrison picked up the hesitant John Hancock and literally
dumped him into the seat of power. As the Founders prepared
to sign the Declaration of Independence, Harrison turned to
the thin Elbridge Gerry of Massachusetts, grinned, and said,
"I shall have a great advantage over you, Mr. Gerry, when we
are all hung for what we are now doing." Given the weight of
his body, Harrison pointed out, he would die quickly while
Gerry would "dance in the air an hour before you are dead."
On a less elevated note, during the war the British published
an intercepted letter they claimed had been written by Benjamin Harrison to George Washington in which The Signer

bragged about his amorous adventure with "pretty little Kate, the Washer-woman's daughter."

William Henry came from the best of Virginia families on both sides—his mother was a relative of Martha Washington and the daughter of Robert Carter, known as "King Carter," one of the richest men in the colonies. But by the time he arrived, the heyday of the family's fortune was over. During the Revolutionary War, the Berkeley mansion was sacked by British troops led by the traitor Benedict Arnold. The boy fled with his mother and youngest sisters. When they returned later, they found that the livestock was gone, and that while the house was still standing intact the interior had been destroyed. According to family legend, when a British nobleman visited Berkeley after the conflict had ended, he noted rather snootily that while the exterior of the great homes of Virginia compared favorably to their English counterparts, their interiors lacked elegant furniture and decor. "I can account for my paintings and decorations, sir," Benjamin roared. "Your soldiers burned them in my backyard."

The Signer suffered from gout with advancing age. His last public appearance was in 1788, when he attended the Virginia convention called to ratify the Constitution. (Benjamin was unenthusiastic, complaining that it still lacked a Bill of Rights.) He was, an observer reported, "elegantly arrayed in a rich suit of blue and buff, a long queue tied with a black ribbon dangling from full locks of snow." Three years later he would be dead, having collapsed after holding a great feast to celebrate his reelection to the Virginia House of Delegates.

William Henry was, at least according to his mother, a "delicate" boy, and he was educated at home until he was fourteen. His older brothers were sent to learn the ways of the world of business and law, but the youngest son was targeted for a career in medicine. It's not clear whether he ever showed any inclination in that direction. Perhaps his father was influenced by his friendship with Benjamin Rush, one of his fellow signers and a prominent Philadelphia physician. But it was also a profession that could provide the boy with a living after a not-too-pricey apprenticeship. Money had become an issue. The Signer had always been more interested in politics than agriculture and, like much of Virginia, Berkeley's overused soil was beginning to erode, producing fewer and fewer crops for a larger and larger family.

At any rate, the youngest son was sent not to the College of William and Mary, where Harrison men had traditionally been educated, but to the small, rustic Hampden-Sidney College, where the curriculum included "the English grammar, Caesar's commentaries, Sallust, Virgil and the Roman Antiquities." Years later, Harrison would say, rather proudly, that he had read Charles Rollin's ponderous histories of Greece and Rome "three times before I was seventeen years old." Later, when he joined the military, he set off to the Indian wars carrying a copy of Cicero. It was a typical education for his day, but it would have a dreadful effect on Harrison's public oratory, which tended to drip with references to Roman generals.

His tenure at Hampden-Sidney was rather short—perhaps the Harrisons, staunch Episcopalians, were disturbed by reports that a spirit of evangelical revival was capturing some segments of the student body. After a brief stay at another school, William Henry was sent to Richmond to study under a doctor, Andrew Leiper. But Richmond, too, had its perils for this young product of plantation society. William Henry fell in with members of the "Humane Society," a group of abolitionists whose leader, Robert Pleasants, had been a political opponent of Benjamin's. (In his diary, Pleasants had recorded the story of Benedict

Arnold's raid on Berkeley and noted with pleasure that the British had carried off forty of the family slaves.) It was probably the closest William Henry Harrison would ever come to flirting with abolitionism. Later, when he became a presidential candidate, Harrison would tell northern supporters that the episode was evidence that he was not pro-slavery, and of course he would discount it entirely when he was in the South.

If nothing else, his exposure to radical thought was brief. Once again, the youngest Harrison was uprooted and transferred to the Medical School of Pennsylvania in Philadelphia. But when he arrived at the city by boat and disembarked in the spring of 1791, he was met by a messenger who informed him that his father had died.

His brothers told him—or at least hinted—that the family could no longer afford to pay for his education, and William Henry quickly began looking for a new career. Since most doctors at the time had little formal training anyway, the fact that he quickly abandoned that line of work does suggest that medicine had never held much attraction. He tried unsuccessfully to get a government job, and then sought advice from Richard Henry Lee, the governor of Virginia, who was visiting Philadelphia at the time. Lee offered him help in getting an army commission. When William Henry expressed a willingness to join the military, President George Washington himself signed off on the commission, saying he "had no reason to reject the request of the son of an old friend."

Some of Harrison's other friends regarded Lee's efforts as less than helpful. The army was at a low point at the time, in terms of both prestige and pay. Fighting the British had given way to fighting the Indians on the western frontier, which most wellborn men regarded as an ignoble occupation—not to mention one that was both extremely uncomfortable and extremely dangerous. But the newly fatherless and somewhat impoverished eighteen-year-old must have felt more than a little desperate. "In 24 hours from the first conception of the idea of changing my profession, I was an Ensign in the 1st US Reg of the Infantry," he wrote later. His biographers have noted that there was actually quite a bit more time spent searching for that desired government post, and one has suggested that the real impetus for Harrison's enlistment was an unsuccessful love affair. But whatever his reasons, he was soon committed to what would become his defining career.

Harrison first became a recruiting officer, staging little parades with a fifer and drummer to draw crowds of passersby with time on their hands, and he managed to sign up eighty men even though at the time army pay was only $2.10 a month—the equivalent of about fifty dollars now. He marched them from Philadelphia to Pittsburgh, where they took off by boat down the Ohio River, Harrison clutching that copy of Cicero. The book must have been a comforting connection to the old days, and also a reminder to himself and those around him that he was a wellborn and well-educated gentleman.

The troops arrived in the fall of 1791 at Fort Washington, a log stockade on the northern side of the river enclosing about an acre of land, at what is now Cincinnati. At the time, it was one of the most western of American settlements, although there actually weren't very many settlers—just twenty-five or thirty cabins clustered near the comforting presence of the military. There were no roads except for Indian trails and virtually no communication with the East except messages carried by the occasional express rider.

It was hardly an opportune moment to begin a military career on the frontier. The Northwest Territory, which included what would later become the state of Ohio, had been roiled by Indian wars, most of which the white Americans seemed to be losing. While Harrison was making his way to Fort Washington, the survivors of a battle to the west were racing through the forests toward the protection of the stockade. Forces under the command of the territorial governor, Arthur St. Clair, had been walloped by the Indian chief Little Turtle in a fight that would come to be known as St. Clair's Defeat. It would go down in history as the worst loss ever to be suffered by white forces in the Indian wars—and in fact, in terms of casualty rate, one of the worst defeats in all of American military history. Little Turtle's men, numbering fewer than five hundred, had killed 630 American soldiers—nearly two-thirds of the total force.

A few hundred men, most of them injured, and a few dozen women, who had followed the army as soldiers' wives, laundresses, or prostitutes, made their way to Fort Washington. There, the pathetic company quickly lost the sympathy of the post commanders. They broke into the village stores and took what they could find, which added up to a small amount of food and a great deal of grog. In his first two days in the West, Harrison said later, he saw more drunken men than he had until then in his entire life.

The following days weren't much better. Harrison discovered that his fellow officers resented him, in part because he had gotten a job that the son of one of the captains coveted, without serving the usual apprentice period as a cadet. The other officers were mainly veterans of the Revolution who had worked their way up in the army, and the arrival of a green former college student wielding a copy of Cicero didn't impress them.

Harrison also soon learned that the army had few horses—as soon as new mounts arrived, the local Indians skillfully stole them. The equipment was poor. Soldiers mainly lived in leaky tents and suffered with faulty guns and poor ammunition. Given the boredom of camp routine, most of the men drank constantly. "At least four fifths of my brother officers died of the effects of intoxication," Harrison claimed later. He grew to dislike drinking, although he would be surrounded by it throughout a life of military encampments and, later, political banquets. When a new commanding officer ordered that any soldier found drunk outside the walls of the fort be instantly given fifty lashes, Harrison enthusiastically followed through. His first target, who was actually a civilian ordnance worker, filed a complaint with the civilian authorities and Harrison was arrested by a local deputy. It was only the intervention of the fort commander that limited Harrison's punishment at the hands of the outraged townsmen to one night in jail.

The only breaks from the dismal circumstances inside Fort Washington were a series of winter marches Harrison was sent on, one of them to try to recover some of the equipment that had been left behind by St. Clair's fleeing troops. The soldiers must have wished they were back in the depressing fort. They trudged through the snow, in freezing rains, and slept exposed to the elements with their saddles for pillows. When they woke up, they often found their hair was frozen to the ground.

Harrison was eventually sent back to Philadelphia, as escort to the wife and children of the fort commander. There, Anthony Wayne, the Revolutionary War hero who was universally known as "Mad Anthony," was busy drilling a new command called the Legion of the United States. (Harrison was far from being the only member of the military obsessed with the ancient Romans.) Wayne had been brought back to duty by his friend

President Washington and charged with whipping the disorganized army into shape.

Harrison joined Wayne's command and was made a lieutenant, but he still yearned for a chance to move upward. Fate intervened when his captain became embroiled in a fight over the affections of a sergeant's wife. Scandal ensued. The captain was whisked away to another post and Harrison was assigned to take his place. Wayne took a liking to Harrison— "a young gentleman of family, education and merit"—and made him his aide-de-camp with a salary of $64 per month. It was a huge raise, even though Harrison's total compensation would have amounted to only about seventeen thousand dollars per year in modern wages.

By then both his parents were dead. William Henry traded the land he had inherited in Virginia for a large parcel the family owned in Kentucky. Like many of his business ventures, it would turn out to be ill advised. The title to the Kentucky land was wrapped up in the complications of frontier surveying, and it would never prove very valuable. But as a symbol it was significant. His Virginia life was over and he looked west for his future.

2

The Governor

The Indian wars in Ohio were triggered by a complaint that William Henry Harrison would hear frequently, and later cause frequently. The white Americans worked under the theory that if they signed an agreement with one tribe that inhabited a territory, it bound all the other people who lived and hunted on the same lands. If the smallest, weakest, greediest, or most desperate group made a deal, even the Indians who had never been involved in negotiations found themselves being pushed out of their traditional homes.

The treaty under which the American government was operating when Harrison came west had been concluded between Arthur St. Clair and some chiefs who the other Indians in the region claimed had no authorization to speak for them. St. Clair rejected the dispossessed Indians' proposal that he meet with their leaders to discuss the matter, and as soldiers began constructing forts in their territory the local tribes formed a confederacy pledged to resist. They believed they could prevail; they had won victories over the white men before and now had the additional advantage of the support of the British, who were still occupying parts of the region that they had promised to leave after the Revolutionary War.

For a while, it looked as if the Indians might be right. "Such sums of money have been thrown away for two succeeding campaigns and nothing effected, but on every account we are worse off than when we began," worried John Cleves Symmes, a leader of the Cincinnati settlers, who would later become Harrison's father-in-law. "I tremble lest Congress should determine that defense of the western country costs the nation more than it is at all worth to them, and leave us to our own defense in the best manner we can make it."

But when Anthony Wayne's forces arrived, the Indians met an enemy that was far better organized and more disciplined than any they had encountered before. The Legion of the United States came down the river to Fort Washington on flatboats and in the fall of 1793 began marching north. By the next summer they had reached a point near what is now Toledo. The force numbered about 3,500, including a large contingent of Kentucky volunteers—men who would win Harrison's affections and test his patience throughout his military career.

The Indian confederacy, led by the Shawnee chief Blue Jacket, was camped near a fort occupied by the still-present British forces. They had taken shelter in a mass of trees toppled by a tornado, and the site would give its name to the battle, which became known as Fallen Timbers. The Indians were taken by surprise, with many of their men away foraging for provisions. The five hundred or so warriors fought bravely, but against hopeless odds, given the fact that their foe was now a disciplined army rather than St. Clair's ill-trained, badly led forces. Eventually the Indians realized they were defeated and fled to the British fort. But the British refused to open their gates to give them refuge. Blue Jacket and the other survivors would never forget that their alleged allies had "dealt treacherously with us" when they most needed them.

During the fighting Harrison, eager to make an impact in his first big battle, rode desperately around the field trying to keep the lines intact, earning the praise of his superiors. (One major wrote that wherever the action was fiercest "there we could see Harrison giving the order.") When it came to danger, the young officer's main concern was keeping his commander out of the line of fire. "General Wayne, I am afraid you will get into a fight yourself and forget to give me the necessary field orders," he told Mad Anthony.

"Perhaps I may and if I do, remember the standing order for the day is, charge the damned rascals with the bayonets," Wayne replied.

In the end, the Indians may have inflicted as many casualties as they took, but the more numerous American whites won the day, ravaging the area and burning the nearby Indian villages. They marched back south, stopping to build a new fort in the area that previously had been at the center of the Indian confederacy's power. They paraded their troops, fired the cannon, and in general made sure to rub in their victory as much as possible. In December, the chiefs came to Fort Greenville, where Wayne was encamped, and asked for peace. The final treaty gave most of Ohio to the Americans for a second time. Harrison was a signer, as were all the white and Indian leaders who fought at Fallen Timbers and survived—with one exception. A young Shawnee chief whose brother had been among the battle casualties boycotted the negotiations and everything to do with the Indians' capitulation. This was Tecumseh, and Harrison would encounter him again.

Harrison returned to Fort Washington, where he would soon be made commander. But first he was assigned to a blockhouse at North Bend, a settlement about fourteen miles west of Cincinnati. There, he had a chance to improve his relationship with Anna Tuthill Symmes, a calm, dark-eyed daughter of Colonel John Cleves Symmes. Anna's mother had died when she was a baby, and she was her father's pet. In a famous family incident during the Revolutionary War, he had disguised himself as a British soldier and crossed the battle lines with his four-year-old daughter to take her to safety with relatives in New Jersey. Anna was comfortable with frontier life, an excellent rider who seemed to have no fears of the dangers of the wilderness. (Her father wrote that his oldest daughter, Maria, who had married and moved to the much more developed city of Lexington, refused to visit the family in Cincinnati because "the fear of the Indians deters her.") Anna was also well read, interested in politics, an eager consumer of newspapers and journals. As a girl, she had been sent to boarding school, where she was a classmate of Martha Washington's granddaughter, and later she would become the first wife of an American president who was known to have been educated outside the home.

She first met her future husband in Lexington, at a party given by Maria and her husband, Peyton Short, a wealthy transplanted Virginian whose family had known the Harrisons back East. When the young Captain Harrison rode up to the Short mansion and saw the lovely Anna Symmes, the two fell into what they assured their children was love at first sight. William Henry found Anna "remarkably beautiful," and she was equally attracted. He had not inherited his father's corpulence. He was a thin man of medium height, with dark eyes and a large, straight nose that dominated his rather ascetic-looking face. He was extremely sociable, and among his generation he had an unusual combination of eastern gentility and western toughness.

Anna was twenty years old when Harrison asked for her hand. Colonel Symmes refused; he was reluctant to give his daughter up at all, and certainly not to a soldier. It's also possible that Symmes—who was one of the civilian authorities during the days when Harrison was a young officer at the fort— had unpleasant memories of the night Harrison was jailed for beating a drunken townsman.

"How do you expect to support my daughter?" he demanded.

"My sword is my means of support, sir!" the young soldier replied, dramatically although not altogether truthfully, since he was already plotting a post-army career.

Romance was going to triumph. Anthony Wayne supported the match, and the wedding took place, although without any help from the father of the bride. Exactly how the Harrisons were married is subject to debate. Some stories suggest that the couple gathered with friends on a day when the colonel was out of town and pulled off a modified elopement, with a ceremony at the home of a friend. Other versions say that Anna was married in her own house, and that her father was present but stalked off in the middle of the ceremony.

At any rate, the family was soon reconciled. Despite his low income, Harrison must have been quite a catch in a frontier settlement where the population numbered only around five hundred. He was a hero of the Indian wars, a protégé of General Wayne himself, well educated, with excellent manners, the product of one of Virginia's best families. And he was looking for a less dangerous and more profitable means of making a living.

Harrison had never had any intention of supporting a family on a soldier's pay after his marriage. He turned his attention to business, even though he was still in the military. He built a gristmill and a sawmill in the nearby Indiana region, and despite his aversion to drink he bought a share in a whiskey distillery. Unfortunately, none of his ventures turned out to be successful. Like many members of the gentry, he seemed to have little talent for business. He had already sold the Tidewater land he had inherited from his father in deals that would net him almost nothing.

The difference between Harrison's generation and the youngest sons of great families in the past was the national conviction that it was possible for any clever man to make great sums of money by his own efforts, without the help of a great inheritance. A much-repeated statistic held that half the rich men in America had started their lives in meager circumstances. This assertion, even if true, would hardly suggest that the chances of a poor boy making a fortune were fifty-fifty, but it gave that impression. The number of young men expecting to rise to the top was large, but except for the rare few who actually did have a talent for business, their hopes were bound to be disappointed. Harrison's era was actually a perilous one for entrepreneurs. The population and the economy were growing, but the American financial system was unstable, given to booms and busts. When great expectations fell flat, if the young man in question was the product of a well-connected family, he would probably turn to the government in search of a well-paying sinecure. Harrison was no exception, and after Fallen Timbers much of his life would be spent struggling to find a good-paying government position to support his ever-expanding family.

The Harrisons moved to a 160-acre farm near the village of North Bend, about fourteen miles from Cincinnati. William Henry purchased the land from his father-in-law, along with a house that John Cleves Symmes had built there. The house was made of logs—a point that would become extremely important in later years. But for its time it was substantial, two stories with three rooms on the ground floor and two rooms on the second. It was set high enough above the river to be floodproof, with commanding views of the Ohio and the territory around it. In 1796, the year following their wedding, Anna gave birth to a daughter, Elizabeth—the first of what would eventually be ten children. Although his family would live well, and sometimes extremely well by frontier standards, Harrison was almost always financially strained. "My nursery grows faster than my strongbox," he once complained.

Harrison stayed in the military until 1798. He became the commander of Fort Washington, although it was then a quiet post, with only about seventy men and not much to do in the peaceful days after the Greenville treaty. He finally resigned his commission and took a job as land registrar and later justice of the peace. Then the office of secretary of the Northwest Territory became vacant, and Harrison threw himself into a letter-writing campaign. "I have been so long in these woods that I have had no opportunity of making myself known to the officers of Government," he wrote to the congressman Robert Goodloe Harper, a powerful Federalist. Harrison humbly noted that he knew very few members of Congress at all—although since one of his handful of acquaintances there happened to be his brother, it's doubtful that he was quite as short on contacts as he suggested.

Harrison was, from an early age, shameless in pursuit of employment that would maintain his family's standard of living. "P.S. I do not know whether I have been very explicit in the above letter," he wrote pathetically at the bottom of his very explicit missive. "I have been for some time extremely ill and am so weak that I can scarcely hold the pen."

He had no compunction about name-dropping. ("From the manner in which I have heard my father speak of the President I am induced to think that there was an intimacy between them," Harrison wrote to Harper about John Adams.) He was also frequently successful. He got the job, which carried a good salary of $1,200 a year.

As secretary, Harrison was conscientious about record keeping and given to the same florid prose that would later mark his important speeches. Run-of-the-mill orders from the governor (the soon-to-be-deposed Arthur St. Clair, who had given his name to that famous defeat) opened with: "His Excellency, the Governor, being at Cincinnati in the County of Hamilton, was pleased to issue the following . . ."

His days of elevated clerical work were brief. In 1799, the territorial legislature elected Harrison its delegate to Congress, where his main job was to support the western settlers on bills relating to the sale of public lands. His great achievement in Washington was the Harrison Land Act, which reduced the size of tracts of land the federal government would sell to as little as 320 acres—half of what had been required before. In another effort to extend the American dream to as many people as possible, the law permitted people to buy land on credit, at two dollars per acre. That greatly expanded the opportunities to acquire farms in the western land, but it also led to a large number of foreclosures.

Harrison also had an opportunity to make new contacts and renew ties to his father's old friends in Philadelphia, which still functioned as the nation's center of government while the new city of Washington was being constructed. The eastern political elite were extremely interested in the unsettled and worrisome West. Everyone wanted to entertain the young delegate who knew both the politics and the military challenges of that mysterious territory—and who, as a bonus, had a lovely wife and good table manners. President Adams in particular was taken with William Henry and invited him to evenings at the White House. Perhaps he saw in the son a thinner and more deferential version of Benjamin the Signer.

When Ohio headed toward statehood, William Henry's presence in Congress made it easier to figure out who should run the new Indiana Territory, which would consist of the land the United States controlled to Ohio's west. President Adams, with the approval of Congress, made Harrison the first governor of the territory, which included most of what are now the states of Indiana, Illinois, Wisconsin, and Michigan. Later, in his presidential campaigns, Harrison would claim that Adams had given him the job to remove an ardent anti-Federalist from the capital, but as delegate to Congress he got along well with the president and had actually been identified with a number of Federalist issues, such as road building and support for creation of a standing national army. It seems more likely that, once again, Harrison was looking for a better salary.

• • •

After all that had already happened in his life, it comes as a shock to realize that William Henry was still only twenty-seven years old when he set off with his family—which by now included three children—for Port Vincennes, the capital of the Indiana Territory. Port Vincennes was two hundred miles from Cincinnati but, since there were no real roads, the only way to reach it during much of the year was an extremely circuitous six-hundred-mile boat trip. Port Vincennes had only about seven hundred residents, most of them descendants of French settlers who had been living in the area for almost a century and who had intermarried with local Indians. Harrison's mother-in-law, reporting on Anna's new home, said it consisted of "460 French and about 40 American families."

Nothing about the Indiana Territory was more than a rough beginning. There were no roads except Indian trails. The government consisted only of the governor himself and three judges. The four of them served as the executive, judicial, and legislative branches, with the power to adopt laws that already existed in other states but not to make up new ones of their own.

It was a brave new world, but the Harrisons had no intention of living like pioneers. In a region full of humble wood-frame houses, sod huts, and log cabins, William Henry built his family a brick mansion, two stories high with thirteen spacious rooms, four large chimneys, carefully hand-carved woodwork, and an imposing semicircular staircase. Everything about it was imported from outside, including the workmen from Ohio and Pennsylvania who were brought in to build it. Harrison sold four hundred acres of land just to raise enough money to buy the bricks. In an era when very few Americans had windows that were anything but holes covered by wooden shutters, Harrison bought window glass from England, an order that took two years to fill.

An adjoining farm, which Harrison had also purchased, produced fruit, vegetables, dairy products, and—thanks to a contingent of pigs—ham and bacon. The governor's mansion quickly became the territorial equivalent of a tourist attraction. No one in Vincennes had ever seen anything like it. It was the sort of place that its inhabitants christen with a name, and Harrison called his home Grouseland.

Harrison would serve as governor for twelve years, during which time he championed improvements such as the establishment of a circulating library, an agricultural society, and public lotteries to support a rudimentary university at Vincennes. On behalf of his many French-American citizens, he petitioned the nearest Catholic bishop for a resident priest and did, at least, acquire a visiting missionary. He lured a printer from Kentucky into town, and with him came a small local paper that was known as the *Indiana Gazette*. But the main job of the territorial governor was not to expand libraries or schools. His chief duty was to acquire land from the Indians for settlers to farm, solidifying the hold of white Americans on the area and eventually turning Indiana into a state. Most non-native people thought this was the right course on every count. As Harrison wrote, it was only proper that "one of the fairest portions of the globe" be put to its best use, rather than wasted in "a state of nature, the haunt of a few wretched savages."

For the national government, the top priority was to secure the boundaries of the nation against the English, the French, and the Spanish—which could be done only with a solid line of settlements. And the settlements would come only when the Indian threat was eliminated. The white Americans also assured one another that their plans were the best thing for the Indians, who would eventually be forced either to take up more civilized lifestyles or to move farther west—to land where no white man would surely ever want to bother going, where the hunting was better and the two races would no longer get in each other's way.

Beyond the grand theories lay the hunger for land to buy and sell. While farming was the way of life for most white Americans, land speculation was the preferred occupation of the elite. Benjamin the Signer had expressed shock "when I reflect on the unbounded thirst of our people after Lands they cannot cultivate, and the means they use to possess themselves of those that belong to others." Many of the Founding Fathers—especially the southern ones—had devoted much of their energies to acquiring vast tracts of land. Harrison's father-in-law, John Symmes, had made his fortune when he and several friends got permission from Congress to purchase roughly 330,000 acres along the Ohio, at a price of about sixty-seven cents per acre. After the government built Fort Washington to protect the incoming civilians, Symmes and his partners sold the land to eager settlers. Unfortunately, their survey work was so sloppy that many settlers found they eventually had to pay for their property a second time.

Harrison became a prodigious signer of treaties. The territory, when he arrived as governor, was a series of small strips along the Ohio River and around Vincennes. Between 1802 and 1805 he acquired what is now the southern part of Indiana, most of Illinois, and parts of Wisconsin and Missouri. Harrison signed seven treaties in all, and he later estimated that he had acquired about fifty million acres of land, at a price of less than two cents per acre. When he was done, he had basically accomplished what the federal government thought at the time was its ultimate goal—pushing the Indian territory beyond the Mississippi River.

Harrison was good at dealing with the Indian leaders. He had watched his superiors negotiate in Greenville after the Battle of Fallen Timbers, and he understood the niceties of the Indian style of bargaining—the long hours of smoking and talking before any discussion of the issues at hand could be broached, the elegant, flowery speeches, the importance of showing hospitality and giving gifts. He did not, under normal circumstances, encourage drinking during negotiations, although

that was a popular tool for white Americans trying to get what
they wanted. Thomas Jefferson, who initiated a regular corre-
spondence with Harrison during these years, suggested that it
might be a good thing to encourage the Indians to run up debt
for supplies or whiskey, "because we observe that when these
debts get beyond what the individuals can pay they become
willing to lop them off by the cessation of lands." After one deal,
in which a group of chiefs agreed to the sale of one and a half
million acres that stretched down the Ohio as far as Louisville,
the Indians were so embarrassed by the bad bargain they had
made that they kept the agreement secret from their people.

At the time, many of the Indians were in dreadful condition. They were weakened by periodic epidemics due to their
inability to withstand bacteria brought into their territories
by the white settlers. And their traditional way of life was dis-
appearing. Settlers' farms had displaced grazing land for game,
and the Indians' own desire for profits from selling pelts had
led to the extermination of much of the local wildlife. The
weaker tribes became dependent on gifts and annuities from
the U.S. government, and they signed treaties turning over
huge swathes of land for as little as a penny or two per acre in
return for the equivalent of welfare payments. (In 1804, when
Harrison briefly had the Upper Louisiana Territory added to
his responsibilities, he attended a ceremony in which he was
greeted by representatives from several of the area's tribes.
When Harrison offered them some food as a sign of friendship, the Indians initially refused, saying that they had heard
that when the Americans gave presents they expected to be
deeded land in return.)

Harrison's dealings with the Indians were not necessarily
helpful to their best interests, but he was at least sympathetic
to their plight. "I wish I could say that the Indians were

treated with justice and propriety . . . by our own citizens but . . . it is very rare that they obtain any satisfaction for the most unprovoked wrongs," he wrote to the secretary of war, who was in charge of Indian affairs. He was painfully aware that while Indians were swiftly punished for committing crimes against whites, it was impossible to get a white jury to convict a white man of killing an Indian. The situation was so stacked, he wrote to Jefferson, that "the name of America has become almost universally odious to the tribes on this frontier." On another occasion, he wrote that "they make heavy complaints of ill-treatment on the part of our Citizens. They say that their people have been killed—their lands settled on— their game wantonly destroyed—& their young men made drunk & cheated of the peltries which formerly procured the necessary articles of Clothing, arms and ammunition to hunt with. Of the truths of these charges I am well convinced."

Harrison's experience as governor also intensified his dislike of alcohol. He attempted to stop white traders from following Indian trapping parties around, giving them liquor and then convincing them to sell for very low prices the skins they had just collected. At one point he issued a proclamation banning the sale of liquor to Indians in the region around Vincennes and he asked the territory legislature to ban the practice completely. The lawmakers acceded—but in a bill that went into effect only when Kentucky, Ohio, and Louisiana followed suit. That, of course, never happened.

However much Harrison might worry about the Indians' plight, he had absolutely no doubt that the treaties were both legitimate and righteous. He worked hard to get the Indians' cooperation, organizing large councils that included both wary chiefs and representatives of friendlier tribes, some of which had little claim to the land in question but whose enthusiasm for a deal helped propel the others along. (Harrison signed one treaty for almost eight million acres in southern Illinois with the tiny Kaskaskia tribe, which consisted of only a few dozen members.) He handed out gifts to those Indians who were cooperative and withheld long-standing annuity payments from those who were resistant. He gave one powerful chief a slave in return for his help and freely doled out what the secretary of war called "pecuniary advances." He treated the chiefs who did what he wanted with a paternal benevolence in which he took pride.

· · ·

Harrison had never owned a large number of slaves, but he was sensitive to the feelings of those who did. "Is there a man vain enough to go to the land of Madison, of Macon and of Crawford," he once asked, naming the great Virginians of the era, "and tell them that they do not understand the principles of the morals and political rights of man; or that, understanding, they disregard them?" Harrison's brief flirtation with the Humane Society as a teenager would be the closest he would ever come to embracing abolition. When he served in Congress he opposed any attempt to stop slavery from expanding into the new territories. However, he often added that he would be sorry if it actually happened.

In his personal life, Harrison had already begun to adopt a practice of purchasing slaves and then making them indentured servants who had the promise of freedom at the end of a specified period of service. He bought a runaway slave named Jack Butler from his master in Kentucky for four hundred dollars and indentured him for twelve years. After completing his service, Butler lived as a free man on a small farm that Harrison owned along the Wabash River. Later, in a campaign for

Congress, Harrison would tell northern audiences that "I have been the means of liberating many slaves but never placed one in bondage."

When Congress banned slavery in the Northwest Territory, Harrison's father-in-law, John Cleves Symmes, was serving as a territorial judge in Ohio and cited that legislation as justification for freeing slaves that had been brought into Ohio from the South. But as governor, Harrison interpreted the law loosely, arguing that while it prohibited the buying and selling of human beings, it did not prohibit slave owners from bringing their slaves into the territory or keeping them once they arrived.

Harrison was aligned with what became known in Indiana as "the Virginia faction" or "the Virginia aristocrats," who saw the ban on slaves as a barrier to growth in the territories. They considered wealthy southern settlers to be the most desirable, and those were likely to be slave owners who would not set down roots in a region where they would be forced to give up their most valuable assets. Two years after his arrival, Harrison petitioned the federal government to allow slaves in the Indiana Territory, arguing that the current regulations had been "the reason for driving many valuable citizens possessing slaves to the Spanish side of the Mississippi."

Congress said no. Harrison and the three judges who served with him then passed a series of laws making it clear that African Americans were not to be considered equal citizens, no matter what their legal status. One law prohibited blacks from testifying against whites in court, and carefully defined "negro" as anyone who had one nonwhite grandparent. Another prohibited nonwhite residents from purchasing white indentured servants, and specified that any "negroes and mulattos" who came into the territory "under contract to serve another in

any trade or occupation" were "obliged to give their masters
their service."

As the territory moved closer to statehood, its residents
were allowed to elect a legislature, and in 1805 the new lawmakers passed an act permitting black and mulatto slaves to
be brought into the territory and registered as indentured servants. But while white indentured servants traditionally sold
their labor, the new black servants did not get any compensation for their work. And most crucially, there was no limit to
the length of servitude—some were registered for indentures
of up to ninety-nine years. The children of these indentured
servants who were born in the territory were supposed to be
freed when they reached maturity. But that "age of maturity"
was defined as somewhere between twenty-eight and thirty-
five. In his private dealings, Harrison was more lenient. When
one of his black indentured servants ran away, leaving behind
two small boys, Harrison had them made apprentices, legally
required to work for the family without pay until they turned
twenty-one. At that time, they were to receive three suits of
clothes, a Bible, and their freedom.

The Indiana system seems on its face a cynical attempt to
maintain slavery under another name, but Harrison did not
regard it that way. In 1804, he intervened in the case of Simon
Vannorsdell, the agent for the heirs of a recently deceased Virginia couple who had brought two slaves, George and Peggy,
when they moved to Indiana. Vannorsdell was trying to take
them outside the territory so he could sell them as part of the
liquidation of the estate. Harrison fought fiercely to protect
George and Peggy, and he issued a proclamation banning the
"nefarious and inhuman" plan to kidnap "colored indentured
servants" for sale as slaves. Peggy was eventually released as
a freewoman but a judge ordered George's case held over

until the next court session. Harrison then put up money for a bond so that George could remain free until the case was resolved. After a long period of litigation, with no resolution in sight, George resolved his own case by indenturing himself to Harrison for eleven years. Even historians who have been critical of Harrison's position on slavery have concluded that, in this case, his purpose was to protect George from being sold, not to secure a new servant for himself.

But Harrison remained aligned with the Virginia faction, and as time went on popular resentment against his pro–slave owner stance grew greater. A bill to repeal the law allowing slaves to be brought into the territory under the disguise of indentured servants passed the popular-elected assembly in 1808 but was killed by the senate, which was comprised of men appointed by the governor. Soon after, the slavery opponents from the Indiana section of the territory formed an alliance with pro-slavery politicians from the Illinois region. Together, they chose a delegate to Congress who succeeded in getting what both sides wanted—the separation of Indiana and Illinois. Harrison, still governor of the Indiana Territory, was stuck with the populist part of his old realm. It was not always a comfortable fit. One of Harrison's longtime opponents, John Badollet, wrote to the secretary of the treasury asking that when the next governor was appointed there be "no more Virginians."

3

Tippecanoe

Harrison would serve as governor of the Indiana Territory for twelve years, acquiring millions of acres of land for the United States, bringing an entire section of the country toward statehood. By the end of his administration, the population of settlers was growing rapidly, and industries like milling, tanning, and distilling were taking hold. The great clouds over the future were the Indians and the British—most particularly the possibility that the two groups most unenthusiastic about American expansionism would form an alliance and try to drive the settlers out of the West.

Indiana depended on its volunteer militias for protection, but Harrison—who had a long-standing belief in the importance of a professional national army—found the volunteers to be unreliable and ill trained. He warned the legislature that the militias needed professional staff to drill the men and decent arms to equip them. This was an issue around which all political factions could rally, and in 1807 the legislature responded enthusiastically, giving Harrison anything he had asked for—including a provision banning black residents from joining the militias.

Leading the militia was the part of governing that Harrison would enjoy most. "Having spent seven years of my life in the army and very much attached to the profession this employment will be by no means unpleasant to me," he wrote to the secretary of war. It was also the part of his early history that would later make him a national politician. When he ran for president, no one would remember anything about the charges of elitism when he was governor or even much about the fights over slavery. His greatest claim to fame would be based on his battle against Tecumseh, his old opponent from Fallen Timbers.

Tecumseh's tribe, the Shawnee, had fallen victim to American treaties back in 1768, when the decimated Iroquois signed over the land that is now Kentucky and western Pennsylvania to the Americans, giving away territory that the Shawnee had long regarded as theirs. They fought, unsuccessfully, against the white settlers' incursion, and one of the warriors who died in those battles was Tecumseh's father, the chief Pucksinwah.

Tecumseh, or Shooting Star, was a remarkable person. "Perhaps one of the finest looking men I ever saw—about six feet high, straight, with large fine features and altogether a daring bold-looking fellow," wrote an officer who had accompanied Harrison to a meeting with the chief. Tecumseh fought his first battle when he was nine, and although he and his six siblings spent much of their childhoods on the run from colonial soldiers, as a young man he befriended a family of white settlers who taught him to read and write in English. He was also reported to speak French. Harrison regarded him as a worthy adversary. "The implicit obedience and respect which the followers of Tecumseh pay to him is really astonishing, and more than any other circumstance bespeaks him one of those uncommon geniuses which spring up occasionally to produce revolutions and overturn the established order," Harrison said. If fortune had not dumped him in the middle of the American progress westward, Harrison theorized, "he would, perhaps, be the founder of an empire that would rival in glory that of Mexico or Peru."

Tecumseh's brother Shawnee Prophet was a less impressive figure. His Indian name was Tenskwatawa, the Open Door, although as a child he had been named He Who Makes a Loud Noise for his incessant crying. Tenskwatawa was clumsy and bad at skills like hunting, so no one expected him to have a future as a warrior. As might have been expected given his low status in the community, he grew up to become an alcoholic. In a drunken stupor, he had a vision in which God told him to save his people from their evil ways. It was a transformative moment, and Tenskwatawa became a medicine man. He started a religious revival movement, urging his followers to avoid alcohol, refrain from overhunting the land, and return to their old customs. It's not always clear where the Prophet's thinking ended and Tecumseh's began, but both brothers believed passionately that the land belonged to all Indians, not one particular tribe, and that it could not be sold. "Sell a country!" said Tecumseh. "Why not sell the air, the great sea, as well as the earth? Did not the Great Spirit make them all for the use of his children?"

By the time he and Harrison met, Tecumseh had given up the affectations of the white man. He wore the deerskin leggings and long, fringed hunting shirts that his forebears had worn, and he decorated his moccasins with dyed porcupine quills rather than the white traders' beads. He did not drink liquor and tried to eat traditional native foods. While the Prophet preached, Tecumseh visited with tribes throughout the region, urging the people to reject leaders who tried to sell their land and inviting the chiefs to join in a great confederacy that would unite to keep Indian territory safe for the Indians.

White leaders, of course, urged their Indian allies to ignore this kind of talk. Harrison suggested that the Prophet's followers demand that he show "some proofs . . . some miracles. . . . If he really is a prophet, ask him to cause the sun to stand still." It was an ill-timed suggestion, since the region was awaiting a solar eclipse, which teams of astronomers had been assembled to watch. The Prophet seems to have known about it, even if Harrison did not. On the appointed hour, he assembled his followers, ordered the sun to go dark, and—it did.

In 1808, the brothers moved into Harrison's territory, establishing a settlement for their followers at the mouth of the Tippecanoe River, in what is now eastern Indiana. The village, Prophetstown, was large by Indian standards, with about two hundred houses, a council house, medicine lodge, and an accommodation for guests called House of the Stranger. The residents, who came from a number of different tribes, cultivated more than one hundred acres and raised a few head of livestock. Alcohol was banned.

Tecumseh insisted that his intentions were peaceful, and in his teachings the Prophet did not talk about a war between Indians and whites. But he did say that God would send some kind of apocalypse that would get rid of the usurpers and leave the land to its rightful owners. That couldn't have left the white people feeling comforted. The settlers were terrified, and they held angry meetings, calling on the authorities to do something about the new Indian town. Rumors spread that the brothers were planning some kind of terrible attack. "The story is that the Shawnee Prophet offers two thousand Beavers for your head," Harrison's father-in-law wrote from Ohio.

More than anything, white Americans in the West were paranoid about a possible alliance between the local Indians and the British, whose presence to the north posed a perpetual source of worry. The Shawnees had a history of working with the British against the Americans, although they also had bitter memories of the treachery after the Battle of Fallen Timbers. Harrison told a friend that the Prophet was "an engine set to work by the British for some bad purpose." And in fact Tecumseh had met with the British in Canada. It was also the British who had tipped off the Prophet to the upcoming eclipse.

Even in the short term, relationships between Prophetstown and the white community were testy. Although Tecumseh and the Prophet ordered their followers to leave the settlers alone, the younger and less disciplined residents of the town had a habit of stealing horses and livestock, and occasionally those forays led to bloodshed. When representatives from the local Indian agent came seeking restitution for the stolen goods, the brothers tried to redirect the government's attention. The Prophet himself went to see Harrison, explaining that his teachings required all races to live together in peace and—in a request that must have won the governor's heart—asking for help in keeping the settlement alcohol free.

The visit seemed to reassure Harrison about the brothers' intentions. Perhaps it was because of the medicine man's unthreatening appearance—he was slight and had lost an eye in a boyhood accident. Talk had been circulating that the Prophet was actually half white—perhaps the illegitimate son of English nobles—and that he had been educated in England. But this unprepossessing Indian was clearly no product of Eton. In fact, he did not seem to pose any danger at all. "Upon the whole Sir I am inclined to think that the influence which the Prophet has acquired will prove rather advantageous," Harrison wrote to the secretary of war.

The era of good feeling did not last very long. New followers continued to arrive at Prophetstown, including about fifty Winnebagos who wanted support for their plans to attack American forts and reclaim land they had lost. Tecumseh, who had only eighty warriors, was not inclined to fight against enormous odds. But there seemed little question that sooner or later a conflict would come, especially if the Shawnee brothers were successful in their well-publicized desire to form a confederacy of all the scattered Indian communities. And the horse stealing continued. In 1810, Harrison sent a message to the Prophet demanding to know whether he wanted a war. "I know your warriors are brave," the governor wrote. "Ours are not less so." And his men, Harrison said pointedly, were far more numerous. He invited the Prophet to a council, but it was Tecumseh who came to the meeting.

Harrison had asked that the Prophetstown delegation be small, but Tecumseh brought a large contingent of warriors, unnerving the whites. Some of the witnesses later said that everything about his arrival seemed designed to throw the Americans off guard. Harrison was sitting with some of his men, including territorial judges and army officers, when Tecumseh arrived, and he genially offered the Indian a chair next to him. Tecumseh declined and sat on the grass, saying that it was the proper place for Indians—"the bosom of their mother." His boldness stunned the group "and for some minutes there was a perfect silence," reported one of the Americans.

For several days, Tecumseh presented his many grievances and his theory that the land belonged to all Indians and not one particular tribe. If the Americans kept taking their land with their wrongful treaties, he said, "I do not see how we can remain at peace with you." Harrison's patient style of negotiation kept the discussions going, but he was used to dealing with far more subservient Indians and did not know quite what to make of this new opponent. Finally, he dismissed Tecumseh's ideas about treaties, arguing that if the Indians had been one nation, the Great Spirit would not have given the tribes different languages.

Tecumseh rose angrily, and his followers jumped to their feet as well. Everyone had agreed to leave their guns behind for the meeting, but the Indians were hardly unarmed, since they'd brought their knives and tomahawks. Some of the white men grabbed fence rails or ran to get reinforcements. Harrison drew his sword, which was more decorative than functional, but then quickly put a halt to the crisis. He coolly announced that the meeting was over. If there was going to be any further discussion between them, it would have to be through intermediaries. That night, Tecumseh sent a message of apology and the council resumed. But nothing was accomplished. There was no middle road between the two men's positions.

As the talks were breaking up, Harrison offered to transmit Tecumseh's demands to the president. Tecumseh responded that he hoped the Great Spirit would give the president wisdom, and "induce him to direct you to give up this land." But, the chief added, the president was far away. "He will not be injured by the war. He may still sit in his town and drink his wine, while you and I will have to fight it out."

Harrison and Tecumseh met once again in 1811, in another fruitless discussion. Then Tecumseh traveled south, to recruit new tribes to his confederacy. While he was gone, Harrison sent saber-rattling messages to the tribes in the region, urging them to warn the Prophet's followers to return to their homes at once. "My warriors are in motion . . . the war-pole that has been raised on the Wabash must be taken down," he told a chief of the Miami tribe.

In the late fall of 1811, Harrison raised about one thousand men and set off on a march toward Prophetstown. Like most forces of the era, it was a somewhat motley collection of raw volunteers along with local militias and members of the standing army. Some of the men who showed up for the march were not even armed. "Volunteers, show yourselves. If Harrison is defeated for want of your help you will have the enemy to fight on your own shore of the Ohio ere long," urged a special edition of the Lexington newspaper in an article entitled "War! War!" (Harrison had not actually been in the military for thirteen years, but there did not seem to be any question that he would be the one to lead the assembled forces.)

Only about a third of Harrison's troops came from the regular army. They were members of the Fourth Infantry Regiment, mainly men from New England, who had been marched across the country, on a trek across the mountains that was "painful in extreme," and then down the Ohio on keelboats. At the other end of the spectrum were the volunteers from Indiana, local men who tended to be undisciplined but fierce in battle. Another large group of volunteers came from Kentucky, led by Joseph Hamilton Daviess, the brilliant and eccentric nephew of Alexander Hamilton. Daviess clearly regarded himself as a leader second only to Harrison on the western frontier, and he gave his men very specific directions about what to bring on their march. They wore blue coats and bear skin caps, and Daviess told them to make sure to bring a large saddle blanket, "fixed with hooks and eyes so as to answer all purposes of a greatcoat in bad weather and either a tent or a bed at night." His own multipurpose blanket was white, and it would prove to be an easy target for Indians in a dawn attack.

The troops that marched from Vincennes were, by the standards of the frontier, an enormous contingent. Harrison rode at the head of the group on his white horse. He wore a calico hunting shirt trimmed with fringe and a beaver-fur hat topped by an ostrich feather. The wife of one of the officers described him as "slender with sallow complexion and dark eyes."

Harrison did not necessarily expect a conflict. The war department in Washington had ordered him to avoid violence if possible, and he may have believed that the Indians would give way and surrender once they saw the size of their opposition. But he certainly had confidence that if the Prophet refused, he could easily level the town and destroy the Indian army. It's hard to say what the rank-and-file soldiers anticipated. Many of the volunteers had never fought in actual combat before.

After a long trek, the soldiers stopped at what is now Terre Haute and built a fort, which Harrison would name Fort Harrison. It was tough work, particularly since the provision boats had lagged behind. After four days of felling logs and drilling, the men were threatening to desert. Harrison told them he understood their grievances and that anyone who wanted to leave was free to do so. For himself, he was receiving the same rations as the soldiers and was prepared to continue the campaign with those who chose to stay with him. The men, mollified, raised their rifles and shouted their support.

Meanwhile, warriors were arriving from other villages to support the forces at Prophetstown if the soldiers attacked. Even as their numbers grew, the Indians remained outnumbered and severely short of ammunition. Tecumseh, before leaving the town, had ordered his brother to resist any temptation to be drawn into combat, and the Prophet would have been well advised to pay attention. But the medicine man either decided that the situation was hopeless and that he had no choice but to make the first move or he believed so strongly in his own magic that he thought he could charm the Americans into surrender. Praying, singing, and dancing, he called on the spirits and then assured the warriors that the white soldiers' bullets would bounce off them like drops of rain.

When the army came within sight of Prophetstown on November 6, Harrison, following his orders, held back his men and waited to see what the Indians would do. Some of the soldiers saw women and children inside the town, and they began to think that perhaps the enemy did not intend to fight after all. Eventually, a delegation of chiefs emerged and proposed that a council be held the next day to resolve their differences. In the meantime, they asked Harrison to draw back a little and make camp, suggesting a site about three-quarters of a mile away, on high ground with water and wood for fires.

Years later, when Harrison became a national political figure, his opponents would claim that he allowed the Indians to lead him into a trap. But the site did appear to be the best possible place for the soldiers to stay. Much more disturbing was Harrison's failure to fortify the camp. He ordered the men to sleep dressed for battle, with their guns next to them. But otherwise there were only pickets and huge campfires built to protect the men against the cold and rain, which made it easy for an enemy to see them. "In common with the whole army I did believe that they would not attack us that night," Harrison later wrote.

But they did, a few hours before dawn. The white soldiers were able to form a defensive line quickly, but they could not really see the enemy. And, silhouetted against their roaring campfires, they were clear targets for the Indians. Harrison could not find his own white horse, which had been carefully tethered to a wagon wheel some distance from his tent. He grabbed the first mount he could find and rode toward the front, where a group of Indiana volunteers who called themselves the Yellow Jackets were bearing the worst of the attack. "Where is your captain?" he asked John Tipton, a semiliterate farmhand who had joined the militia to avenge his father, who had been killed by Indians when Tipton was a child.

"Dead," said Tipton.

"And your lieutenants?"

"Dead."

Tipton, an ensign, was the only officer who remained alive. Harrison put him in command.

The misadventure with his horse may have saved Harrison's life. As he rode toward the line of fire he was joined by his aide-de-camp, Colonel Abraham Owen, a leader of the Kentucky militia who had been one of the few survivors of St. Clair's Defeat. Owen had a white horse of his own, and he was quickly shot dead. The soldiers later theorized that the Indians had been waiting for an officer on a white horse to come toward them and took immediate aim, thinking they were looking at Harrison. Or it could simply have been that anything white was easy to spot in the dark. Joseph Daviess, the commander of the Kentucky volunteers with the big white horse blanket, did not last long either.

Harrison behaved as he normally did in battle, moving quickly and calmly to keep his men in proper formation. At the end of the fighting he was unhurt, although a bullet left a hole in the brim of his hat. Once light came and the soldiers could see where they were firing, they quickly got the upper hand. The Indians fled, and the soldiers rode into Prophetstown and leveled the village, destroying everything they could not easily take with them on the march back to Vincennes.

"The Gov. Returned thanks for our good conduct," wrote Tipton, who would be hailed as a hero when he returned home, elected county sheriff, and then propelled onward and upward from one office to the next until he wound up in the U.S. Senate. There, he was made chairman of the Committee on Indian Affairs. Tippecanoe turned out to be a career maker for more than one American politician.

4

The War of 1812

When the soldiers from the Fourth Infantry Regiment returned to Ohio, they marched into Cincinnati under an arch inscribed "To the Heroes of Tippecanoe." The westerners were nervous about the future and eager for good news to cheer about, and most of them were happy to regard the Battle of Tippecanoe as a big victory.

Gradually, that became the consensus, and Harrison would become known as the hero of a battle with Tecumseh in which Tecumseh was not actually present. But the early reactions to Tippecanoe were decidedly mixed. Harrison's forces suffered 188 dead and wounded, far more than the Indians, and casualties had fallen disproportionately on the higher-ranking elite, such as Kentucky's Joseph Hamilton Daviess. Their survivors wanted to know why Harrison had not made more of an effort to fortify a camp he knew was vulnerable to attack. And while Harrison had burned Prophetstown, he had failed to kill or capture many Indian warriors. The young braves scattered all over the region, attacking settlers, stealing horses, and doing general damage. Soon Tecumseh, who as Harrison knew was far away at the time of the attack, would ally with the British in Canada—the very outcome the federal government had most feared.

But Harrison got support from many of his fellow soldiers and, most importantly, from the administration of James Madison. The president himself praised "the collected firmness which distinguished their commander on an occasion requiring the utmost exertions of valor and discipline." And residents of western settlements, who wanted to believe they were being made safer, celebrated. "The Blow Is Struck," rejoiced the Lexington paper, *Liberty Hall*.

The Battle of Tippecanoe was fought on November 7, 1811. By the next summer the country would be at war with Great Britain, with bigger matters to debate.

. . .

Westerners thought of the War of 1812 mainly in terms of the Indians, and even those in the remote parts of the frontier expected to be deeply involved in the conflict. In his first address to the Indiana Territory's legislature in 1807, Harrison had said that if war came, the settlers would bear the brunt, for "who does not know that the tomahawk and scalping knife of the savage are always employed as the instruments of British vengeance."

Easterners barely connected the Indian question with the new conflict that the country was lurching into. The British, at war with Napoleon's France, were blocking American trade, boarding American ships, impressing American sailors, and injuring American pride. "The blood rises to my cheek when I reflect on the humiliating, the disgraceful scene, of the crew of an American ship of war mustered on its own deck by a British Lieutenant, for the purpose of selecting the innocent victims of their own tyranny," Harrison wrote after the HMS

Leopard attacked and boarded the American frigate *Chesapeake.*

Although he would continue to draw his pay as governor into 1813, when war came Harrison for all practical purposes left Indiana and rejoined the army. The rapidly expanding legend of Tippecanoe had won him many fans in Washington, the most important of whom was Henry Clay, the young Speaker of the House from Kentucky, who was an icon to western voters.

"No military man in the U. States combines more general confidence in the West," Clay wrote to Secretary of State James Monroe. "I hope the President will find it proper to bestow on him one of the Brigadiers' appointments lately authorized."

The first set of those appointments proved to be a disappointment. The administration passed over Harrison, showing a preference for Revolutionary War veterans such as William Hull, the governor of the Michigan Territory. Hull was told to recruit an army to march to Detroit, while another westerner, James Winchester of Tennessee, was to raise an army in Kentucky in case Hull needed support.

Harrison, who was always prepared to press his own case, traveled to Cincinnati in the summer of 1812, theoretically to visit his family. Despite the danger of Indian attacks that he had been warning about for some time, he seemed in no hurry to return to Indiana, even when President Madison officially declared the nation to be at war with Great Britain. Writing to Secretary of War William Eustis, Harrison said that there was "no immediate necessity" for him to return home to his official post at Vincennes. He was working his contacts hard, particularly Charles Scott, the governor of Kentucky. Harrison urged Scott to write to Madison and tell the president that he was popular with Kentucky officers and would serve well as a leader of the state's volunteers.

That was certainly true. Harrison had the sense of command that was natural to a member of the national elite, along with the informality and simplicity that came from life as a soldier and frontiersman. Despite his lifelong attachment to verbose speeches with complicated classical allusions, Harrison was an easy man to like, especially for the rough soldiers who were frequently bullied about by their commanders. One soldier described him as someone "in whose company we cannot but be perfectly at ease." Harrison also understood the temper of the Kentucky volunteers—that they were eager to show up for a fight but loath to commit themselves to a set period of service, and that they were brave in battle but hard to discipline, especially when it came to restraining them from going on the attack, whether the time was right or not. Kentuckians, Harrison said in a rare show of irony, were the only men he had cause to complain about for being overenergetic.

Governor Scott complied with Harrison's request to write to the president, but despite his efforts, and lobbying by Henry Clay, Secretary Eustis seemed to prefer leaving Harrison where he was.

Luckily for Harrison's fortunes, if not for the progress of the war, General Hull turned out to be a disaster who wound up surrendering Detroit to British troops—and their Indian allies, led by Tecumseh. The ominous news from the north created a crisis atmosphere in Kentucky. State leaders, urged on by Clay, advised Governor Scott to appoint Harrison major general of the state militia with orders to go to the aid of Detroit. As Clay admitted in a letter to James Monroe, Scott actually had no authority to make such a move. But he pointed to the emergency of the situation.

Thus encouraged, Harrison went to Cincinnati, where General Winchester was camped, on his way to relieve Hull. The troops included one regiment of regular enlisted men and three regiments from the Kentucky militia. Harrison announced he was taking the Kentucky forces. Winchester was understandably outraged.

By then, the Americans had learned that Detroit had fallen, and the Indians were flocking to throw in with what seemed like an inevitably victorious British army. Large parts of the Indiana Territory were either under siege or in a state of general panic. It was an inappropriate moment for squabbles over rank and position, but the fighting over who was in control of the northwestern army went on. Harrison wanted desperately to rescue Detroit and protect his country, but he was far less eager to assist some other general in doing it. Eventually, Harrison received his official appointment as a brigadier general, and then later, after a great deal more negotiating, he was given the command he sought.

Precious time had been lost, however, and by the time Harrison had consolidated his authority it was September. The newly minted general decided to move his army north in three sections, and then regroup for the attack on Detroit. Marching north in the dead of winter, Harrison guarded his supply lines by razing the Indian villages along the route. The homes belonged to the Miamis, old allies of the Americans, and the most the general did to protect his former friends was to recommend that certain chiefs who had gone the extra mile to keep the peace be protected—although, he added to his subordinates, "it is not my wish that you should run any risk in saving those people."

Getting supplies to the far-flung troops in bad weather, over territory that was almost entirely roadless, with rivers made impassable by ice and one thirty-five-mile stretch aptly named Black Swamp, was a logistics nightmare. Harrison was responsible for procurement along with his other myriad duties, but the contractors he had inherited were in many cases overwhelmed or inept. Food was scarce, as were blankets, boots, and everything else the men needed to protect themselves from the cold and wet. In forces that were made up mainly of militia volunteers, desertions were rampant. General Winchester, leading one section of the troops, faced a near mutiny by his hungry men, which was averted only by the sudden delivery of a pack of hogs.

As Harrison eventually recognized, the winter campaign was a bad idea, and the Madison administration seemed worried. But when disaster came it fell on General Winchester, who reached the proposed meeting point on the Sandusky River in January, then decided to march thirty-five miles farther and rescue the inhabitants of the village of Frenchtown, on the Raisin River, which was under British control. He took the town with three hundred men and expected to be able to stay there until reinforcements arrived. But Harrison's other wings were bogged down and British forces under Colonel Henry Proctor got there first. Winchester himself was captured by Indians under the command of the Wyandot chief Roundhead, and surrendered his army. Proctor, fearing Harrison's arrival, left with his own troops, the wounded British, and the American prisoners who were able to march. He left the other eighty wounded Americans in the keeping of his Indian allies. The Indian guards killed thirty of the men in a gruesome manner, and were stopped only when Tecumseh, who got word of the massacre that was under way, rushed back to the scene and intervened on the prisoners' behalf.

The Americans focused not on Tecumseh's efforts at saving white soldiers but the atrocities that preceded his arrival. "Remember the Raisin!" became an American battle cry. Word reached Washington, D.C., that one of the victims was Captain Nathaniel Hart, Henry Clay's brother-in-law. Although only slightly injured, Hart was unable to make the long march with the able-bodied prisoners and bribed one of the Indian guards to get him a horse and help him escape. The Indian complied, but Hart was shot and scalped as he fled.

Harrison had left his army at Fort Meigs, in the Ohio interior, while he tried to recruit new volunteers and improve the supply lines. To some of his critics, that looked like a dereliction of duty. A few made wild charges that he had allowed the disaster at Raisin River to occur because he wanted to remove a competitor in General Winchester. These accusations, along with complaints about his failure in 1811 to secure the camp at Tippecanoe, would be resurrected later—the more prominent Harrison became, the more his political opponents would second-guess his previous military decisions. But by the end of the long winter most Americans, including the command in Washington, seemed eager to believe that the army in the Northwest was under the command of a competent and possibly heroic general.

Harrison's plans worked out. He was aided in part by the fact that the British commander Proctor was given to delay and indecision. The British could have attacked Fort Meigs while Harrison was gone, but Proctor delayed, waiting for the arrival of Tecumseh and his warriors. By the time the British were ready, Harrison was back in the fort, well stocked with provisions, and was able to withstand the assault despite the loss of a large number of the Kentucky troops sent to reinforce his position.

In the fall of 1813, American fortunes improved greatly with the defeat of the British navy on Lake Erie by Commander Oliver Perry. Harrison and his forces retook Detroit and went in pursuit of the fleeing British. His men were joined by mounted volunteers led by Colonel Richard Mentor Johnson, the brave and eccentric Kentuckian who Harrison would encounter on later political battlefields. They overtook the retreating Colonel Proctor and Tecumseh at a point along the Thames River.

The ensuing Battle of the Thames was another confusing, messy encounter in which Harrison had the advantage of greatly outnumbering his enemy. The British army was already in retreat at the time, and it was Tecumseh who persuaded Proctor to make what the great Indian chief must have known would be his final stand. Harrison had 3,500 troops. The British had only 800 men, plus 500 Indian allies. The result was a foregone conclusion. Instead of attacking in the classic way, in long extended lines, Harrison let his mounted backwoodsmen go at the enemy en masse. The British lost heart quickly and fled or surrendered.

The Indians fought on, hoping to at least delay the American advance until their women and children were able to flee. Colonel Johnson tried to draw the Indians' attention away from the main American force by leading about twenty of his horsemen in a charge. They were stopped by Tecumseh and his men, whose gunfire killed or wounded fifteen of the American cavalrymen. Johnson, who was hit five times, continued the fight, and at some point during the battle Tecumseh was killed.

That ended both his warriors' heart for fighting and any hope of a confederation of Native Americans to resist the constant white incursion on their lands.

The question of who killed Tecumseh was never resolved. It was not Harrison, who was nowhere near the site of the chief's death. It could conceivably have been Johnson, who fought hand-to-hand with one Indian warrior, in a battle that left the Indian dead and Johnson gravely wounded. Johnson himself never claimed that his opponent was Tecumseh, but the legend that he was the man who brought down the dreaded warrior was the making of his future political career.

The Kentucky soldiers did find a body that they believed was Tecumseh's, but they mutilated it so grossly that Harrison refused to let his British captives try to identify him. The Americans had skinned the corpse, dividing up the strips of flesh as souvenirs. Harrison was, as he said later, "mortified" by what had happened, and although he quickly reported to his superiors in Washington that the battle had been won, he made no mention of Tecumseh's death. The Americans followed up their victory by burning down Moraviantown, the home of the Munsee Indians, a peaceful tribe that had converted to Christianity and had nothing whatsoever to do with the war.

Tecumseh had symbolized Native American resistance, and white Americans were euphoric at the news of his death. In New York, City Hall was draped with a picture of Harrison accepting the surrender of the Indian chiefs. William Henry was a military hero second only to Andrew Jackson in the nation's heart.

But Jackson came out of the war a national icon, while Harrison became a retiree.

• • •

The country was eager to celebrate Harrison's service, and he undertook a tour of major cities, each of which feted him with a banquet that featured, as was then the custom, endless rounds of alcoholic toasts. Meanwhile in Washington, Madison's new secretary of war, John Armstrong Jr., was plotting to push Harrison out. His motives don't seem to have been much deeper than a desire to make room for some of his own preferred candidates for top army posts. He started pestering Harrison by auditing his payments to contractors and generally trying to make the sensitive general as miserable as possible.

It was a difficult time for Harrison. His father-in-law, John Cleves Symmes, had died and left William Henry in charge of his estate, which was in chaos due to those ongoing problems with surveying the massive amounts of property Symmes had acquired from the government.

"He had come into the wilderness with a patent for a million acres," one of Harrison's most admiring biographers wrote forgivingly of Symmes. "These he had to survey, to sell and to start the machinery of civilization. For ten years there was constant danger from Indians, many of the settlers were irresponsible, the surveyors were careless or incompetent and there were overlapping boundaries. So that sometimes Judge Symmes sold what he did not own or at other times he sold 100 acres and the buyer was given 150 acres. It was impossible to keep exact records and for years General Harrison . . . had all manner of troubles."

In May 1814, with the war still raging, the beleaguered Harrison, his pride wounded, sent Madison a letter asking him to accept his resignation. It's possible that Harrison expected that the president would refuse to let him go and order Armstrong to back off. But the secretary of war cannily intercepted the letter and accepted the resignation on Madison's behalf.

Although Madison did not attempt to intervene when he discovered what Armstrong had done, he did ask Harrison to accept a different commission and negotiate postwar treaties with the tribes in the West. The request was full of praise for Harrison, and it may have gone some way to soothing his feelings, even though holding councils with the Indians did not have anything like the prestige of leading an American army. But Harrison agreed. He negotiated his last treaties and then returned to Ohio. At the age of forty-one, his military career was over.

5

Pursuing a Post

The Ohio to which Harrison returned in 1814 was still raw, but its people were no longer struggling to claw out a meager living in the wilderness. The dirt paths that left farmers stranded in mud for most of the year had begun to give way to more efficient roads—in particular the great National Road that would eventually stretch from Maryland to Illinois. Along with the Erie Canal, which would soon connect the Great Lakes to the Atlantic Ocean, it was the beginning of a network of roads and waterways that would allow farmers and merchants in states like Ohio to transport produce and wares across half a continent. Meanwhile soldiers returning east from the war brought word of the rich possibilities of the region, prompting an influx of new settlers. By the time Harrison returned to Congress in 1816, Ohio would be the fifth most populous state in the Union.

"I am Settled here I believe for life—With as Good a prospect of Happiness as any person Can have," he wrote to a friend. He was forty-one, and his ninth child, a daughter, had just been born. (The Harrisons would have one more child, who would die as a toddler.) The family also included the daughter

of a friend who was killed at Tippecanoe and the son of a doctor who had served with Harrison. Both were taken in and
raised as part of the family. William Henry devoted himself to
his farm and to writing letters on behalf of former soldiers who
needed money, medical care, or—most often—jobs. Championing America's veterans had always been, and would always
be, his passion.

Harrison moved his family back into the home overlooking
the Ohio River's north bend that he had built after his
marriage. But while the original two-story log "cabin" was
retained, it was plastered over, improved, and expanded into a
sixteen-room clapboard house, surrounded by nearly three
thousand acres of land, which included a formal garden and
an orchard. The only actual hint of a log was in one bedroom
closet, where the original wood was left exposed out of nostalgia. In the neighborhood it was known as the Big House,
and it included two large halls and an expansive kitchen with
a brick oven and fireplace that covered one entire wall. It was
not a mansion by the standards of the Virginia plantation culture from which Harrison emerged, but it was comfortable
and commodious—as would have been necessary for a man
with a large family and a reputation for unstinting hospitality.
"He kept an open table to which every visitor was welcome,"
wrote a Congregationalist minister who stayed with the general and his wife. "The table was loaded with abundance and
with substantial good cheer, especially with the different kinds
of game." Game might have been the main meat staple, but
the family and guests devoured an average of one entire ham
per day.

The people sitting around Harrison's table, family and guests
alike, managed to consume most of what his farm produced.
He kept trying to expand his income by investing in one busi

ness or another—an exporting company, a foundry. None of them did well, and Harrison would be forced to borrow against his land to maintain the standard of living at which he expected to raise his children and entertain his friends.

"He is a small and rather sallow-looking man who does not exactly meet the associations that connect themselves with the name of general," the visiting minister reported. But he added that there was "something imposing in the dignified simplicity of his manners" that made an excellent impression. While Harrison became controversial in his various political activities, he was always personally popular in any society in which he traveled. One of his archenemies in Indiana Territory politics, Isaac Darneille, praised his "handsome manners" and added that "in conversation he is sprightly and gay." In southern Ohio, he was far and away the most prominent citizen, continually invited to dedicate new public buildings, to give speeches in honor of national holidays, and to receive his fellow Cincinnatians' good wishes at endless dinners. Most of these dinners were all-male affairs that went on for hours and featured so many toasts it is a miracle anyone was in condition to ride home afterward. Harrison, despite his many reasons to dislike alcohol, was hardly a teetotaler. Virtually everyone drank in his era, when water and milk were often of suspect purity and people routinely drank cider, beer, or hard liquor with their meals. A man—particularly an old soldier—who abstained would have been regarded as, at minimum, eccentric.

Harrison's fellow citizens readily nominated him for office whenever suitable openings arose. In 1816 he was appointed to fill the seat of a local congressman who had resigned, and he was simultaneously nominated for the post in the next election as representative from Indiana. (North Bend was close enough to the border to allow him to serve in both states.) The nomination was not a very dramatic moment. The office was filled and the ticket for the next election put together by twenty-nine men meeting in a country tavern. And the campaign was not much more exciting. "There was no speech making in this campaign and except for a letter in defense of General Harrison it is impossible from the newspapers to make out that a campaign was in progress," said a biographer.

Harrison was eager to get to Washington, in part because he wanted to tamp down rumors that he had received kickbacks from the commissaries he employed to get supplies to his troops during the War of 1812. A select committee was looking into the charges, under the leadership of Senator Richard Mentor Johnson of Kentucky, the former colonel who had possibly killed Tecumseh at the Battle of Thames. There was also gossip about Harrison's performance on the field, and the Senate had tabled a resolution offering the nation's thanks, and a gold medal, to the retired general. "You must spare no pains to get into Congress," Governor Isaac Shelby of Kentucky wrote to Harrison. A former aide added his urging, arguing that as a congressman "you can then meet the insinuations made by your enemies upon an equal footing and by confronting them, establish for yourself a fame which cannot be effected by their base slander."

During his brief time as a congressman, Harrison devoted most of his efforts to military affairs, pushing successfully for pensions to the widows and orphans of militiamen who had fallen in the line of duty. He had less success with another long-term cause, the establishment of universal military training for all young American men. Harking back once again to ancient Rome and Greece, he said that "the whole secret of ancient military glory—the foundation of that wonderful combination of military skill and exalted valor which enabled the petty Republic of Athens to resist the mighty torrent of Persian invasion; which formed the walls of Sparta and conducted the Roman legions . . . to the conquest of the world, will be found in the military education of youth." His colleagues remained unmoved.

Harrison also fought for protection for settlers who had difficulty paying the debt on land they had purchased from the government because of the complications of the nation's disorganized system of competing banks and banknotes. "The Western people are asked to pay in money which is obtainable," he said, arguing for extensions. During a debate on the admission of Illinois as a new state, Harrison declared himself opposed to slavery. But whenever the question of whether to prohibit slavery in new territories or states arose, he voted with the southerners—even though his own constituents would probably have preferred him to side with the anti-slavery faction.

While he was in Washington, Harrison returned to his childhood home at Berkeley for a sentimental visit and the inevitable dinner. (His brothers were both dead, and the plantation had been passed on to a nephew named, inevitably, Benjamin VII.) At the dinner Harrison fell back on his everready store of classical references and told the guests that "to be feasted in the prytaneum of their native city was the greatest reward which an Athenian general could receive."

When his two-year term ended, Harrison did not run for reelection, returning to Ohio and his family duties in 1819. ("Our debts are extremely large and pressing," he wrote.) However, he did allow his supporters to nominate him for the state senate, a much less demanding job. Once again, another delegation met in a country tavern and the matter was sealed. The nomination was supposed to be the equivalent of election, but a second ticket arose from the anti-bank forces, who opposed Harrison as a man who "is not known to be an enemy of banking and he is a director of the branch at Cincinnati."

The bank controversy was very much a product of its time, although the consequences will sound familiar. After the War of 1812, the country's confidence in its western expansion boomed, and with it land prices and speculation of every type. Inevitably, the bubble burst. Ohio in particular suffered and, rightly or wrongly, people tended to blame the government-chartered United States Bank and its branches for their miseries. Harrison had once been a director of the Cincinnati branch and had been active in the banking business. But he voted in Congress for the repeal of the act that had created the bank, and he ran for the state legislature as "the enemy of banks in general and especially the bank of the United States."

Earlier in the year of 1819, the state legislature had vented its wrath on the United States Bank of Ohio by levying astronomical new taxes on each branch. When the banks resisted, the state auditor seized one hundred thousand dollars from one as payment. The bank sued, and the case would eventually make its way to the Supreme Court, which in 1824 would declare the Ohio tax unconstitutional. But it was pretty evident which way the ruling would go, since an attempt by Maryland to do something similar had already been rejected by the Supreme Court in the landmark case *McCullough v. Maryland.*

Harrison won his election, presenting himself in the campaign and later in the state senate as an anti-bank man. But he always insisted that the Supreme Court, right or wrong, had the final say in such matters. As a state senator, he had some success in curbing the Ohio legislature's more extreme attempts to vent populist wrath against the bank and its branches.

He tried to steer a middle road, too, on the issue of slavery, with less result. A resolution urging Congress to prohibit Missouri from joining the Union as a slave state passed, despite Harrison's attempts to water it down, and he voted in opposition.

In his single term in the state legislature, from 1819 to 1821, Harrison also pushed his long-standing crusade for improvements in the militia and proposed a bill to establish public schools. Then he returned again to North Bend, in what appeared to be the end of his political career. He tried several times to be elected to higher office, and suffered a series of embarrassing losses, including one failed bid for governor and two for Congress. Finally, in 1825 Harrison was returned to Washington by the state legislature, which chose him to be one of Ohio's two U.S. senators. There, he was a supporter of President John Quincy Adams and an advocate of federal funding for a national infrastructure, especially in the form of roads. "I have seen a great deal of human misery," he said. "But I have never seen it in any shape which touched my heart in greater degree than in the emigrants to the Western Country before the Cumberland Road was constructed."

Harrison spent three years in the Senate, during which time he continued his persistent search for more lucrative government appointments. When John Quincy Adams ran for reelection in 1828, he tried unsuccessfully to get the vice presidential nomination, which went instead to Secretary of the Treasury Richard Rush—the son of Benjamin the Signer's old friend the Philadelphia physician. Harrison then sought a diplomatic appointment, first as the U.S. minister to Mexico and then to Colombia.

"This person's thirst for lucrative office is absolutely rabid," President Adams wrote. "Vice-president, major-general of the Army, Minister to Colombia—for each of these places he has been this very session as hot in pursuit as a hound on the scent of a hare." Harrison had, Adams admitted, a wide circle of friends who were urging his appointment. But the president judged the applicant "a political adventurer," with "a lively and active, but shallow mind." At a cabinet meeting, however, Adams found himself outnumbered by Harrison's supporters, and he reluctantly gave in.

"Harrison wants the mission to Colombia much more than it wants him, or than it is wanted by the public interest," the frustrated president complained to his diary.

Harrison certainly wanted the mission, which carried a salary of nine thousand dollars per year. He was deeply in debt and was concerned about his grown sons, at least one of whom had already gotten himself into serious financial trouble. "My great object is to save a little money," he wrote a friend.

Besides, the distinction of the appointment was great. Colombia in the mid-nineteenth century included the present-day countries of Venezuela and Ecuador, and it was ruled by Simón Bolívar, the great hero who had liberated his people from Spanish colonial rule. Harrison happily set off for South America, bringing his eighteen-year-old son Carter as attaché. He had never been outside the country before, save his military forays into Canada. He had no diplomatic experience, unless you count his dealings with the Indians. And time would show him to be a rather naive, although well-intentioned, minister.

It took Harrison nearly a year to get to Bogotá, partly due to delays in his preparations. The trip itself involved a long and stormy trip at sea, followed by a series of overland journeys culminating in a forty-day trek through the Andes. Once the party arrived, it would take six months for regular mail from friends and family to reach them.

Harrison complained that his dishes and silverware had vanished during the long and painful trip, and he disliked the climate in Bogotá, but his naturally gregarious character soon won him a wide circle of friends. (Bolívar's minister of foreign relations called him "a simple and good man . . . more of a countryman than a diplomat.") Harrison rented an impressive home and spent a great deal of his time gardening. A clerk at the legation wrote, "When a dinner is given by any of the Diplomatic Corps he is always called upon for his vegetables."

Raising vegetables was the biggest achievement Harrison would have time to accomplish. Andrew Jackson's triumph in the presidential election of 1828 made it inevitable that Harrison's days in Bogotá were numbered, but Jackson acted more speedily than anyone had expected. In March 1829, four days after his inauguration, he appointed a successor, Thomas Patrick Moore of Kentucky. It was one of the first appointments Jackson made, and Harrison's friends took it as proof that Jackson preferred to be the only military hero in American public life.

Even some of Jackson's friends were shocked at the speed with which Harrison was removed. Legend has it that William Barry, Jackson's new postmaster general, protested Harrison's inglorious sacking. Barry had served under Harrison in the War of 1812. "If you had seen him as I did, at the Battle of the Thames, you would, I think, let him alone," he told Jackson.

"You may be right, Barry," the president retorted. "I reckon you are, but thank God, I didn't see him there."

Jackson may have acted out of the simple desire to make room for a favorite. But he was a man with a long memory, and probably had not forgotten about a vote that Harrison had cast during his term in Congress. The question involved whether to censure Jackson for having executed two men in 1818 during his war against the Seminoles in Florida. The great majority of the House members voted against censure; a minority voted yes. But only Harrison tried to split the difference and exonerate Jackson for one death while censuring him for the other.

Harrison's brief stay in Colombia nonetheless turned out to be an eventful one. Bolívar, who had led the fight against Spanish colonial rule with the dream of creating an American-style democratic republic, found his *Gran Colombia* too impoverished and fractious for the model and began exercising more dictatorial powers while his opponents plotted an insurrection. Harrison sent reports to Washington of the plots and counterplots, with detail that made it pretty plain he was in the confidence of Bolívar's enemies. There was no evidence that he was actually plotting with the conspirators, but his own views of the rightness of the American form of government and the evils of one-man rule made it inevitable that his sympathies would lie in that direction.

When his replacement arrived, Harrison sent one final missive to Bolívar, which would be circulated during the presidential campaign of 1840. After some assurances of goodwill and friendship, it veered off into a lecture about the government's tilt toward dictatorship. "Are you willing that your name should descend to posterity amongst the mass of those whose fame has been derived from shedding human blood, without a single advantage to the human race? Or shall it be united to that of Washington as the founder and the father of a great and happy people?" Harrison demanded.

The letter did more good as a document for distribution in

future political campaigns than it did when it was given to Bolívar. While Harrison and his party were touring the country and visiting friends before their departure, the Colombian government was preparing charges that Harrison, his son, and several other diplomats had plotted with the insurrectionists. Nothing came of the controversy but a great deal of confusion, and the Harrisons hastily left for home.

The unceremoniously recalled diplomat made his way to the port of Cartagena, where he was stranded for weeks in one of the more uncomfortable cities in the region, until he was rescued by a New York merchant, Silas Burrows, who put his ship at Harrison's disposal. It was a gesture that earned him a lifelong friend. "If you had not arrived here," Harrison wrote, "I do not know how I should have reached home—I offer you a most hearty farmer's welcome should you ever visit Ohio, in which State at North Bend I shall probably spend my remaining days." Harrison was able, of course, to eventually do much better and Burrows was a guest at the White House when he was inaugurated.

Harrison returned to Ohio after a nineteen-month absence with nothing to show for his South American sojourn but a working knowledge of Spanish, a pet macaw, and a need for cash. The failure of his latest business venture, an iron foundry, had left him deeply in debt. A flood in 1832 caused considerable losses, as did a summer drought. Harrison had long since sold the land he had inherited from his parents and the New Jersey property Anna had inherited from her mother. The North Bend farm, which ran for about five miles along the river, beginning at the Indiana border, was also being continually sectioned off as Harrison gave parcels to his daughters when they married and large chunks to two of his sons. His own farming never managed to support the family, even when the weather was good. ("Money is very scarce and hard to be got," Anna had written to one of her sons.)

As his five sons entered adulthood, most of them presented a financial drain. John Cleves Symmes Harrison, the oldest son, stayed on in Indiana, living in the Grouseland mansion for a decade after his father decamped. During that time he worked for the federal land office, an appointment that had caused some political controversy during his father's many campaigns. More crucially, he fell into economic disaster when he cashed a draft—the equivalent of a check—for five thousand dollars for a friend who turned out to be not only penurious but saddled with other debts that wound up on John Cleves's shoulders, to the tune of twelve thousand dollars. Not long after Harrison returned to Ohio, John Cleves's family was hit with typhoid fever that carried him off, leaving a widow and six children. William Henry and Anna brought them to their home to nurse them back to health, adding seven more mouths to their list of dependents. The general then traveled to Washington to ask his old fellow Indian fighter Richard Mentor Johnson for assistance in getting John Cleves's widow out from under her late husband's debt. Johnson proved extremely helpful, and while the debt itself was not wiped away, the widow was given eighteen years to pay it back, without interest penalties.

Meanwhile William Henry Jr., the second son, was attempting to live as a farmer on land the elder Harrison had given to him, but a drinking problem kept landing him in financial troubles as well. "I will set myself to work to renovate your Fortunes," his father promised, but the young man proved unredeemable and his farm was eventually given over to a tenant. And the second-youngest, Benjamin, would turn out to be one of the less fortunate bearers of the name. He had earned a medical degree, but his inclinations were more toward adventure than medicine. The general complained that Benjamin had returned from a trapping expedition out west more than one thousand dollars poorer than when he embarked.

"I have sold so much of my property that should I be obliged to sell as much as would clear me of debt, I should be left without the means of supporting the large family, or properly families, which are dependent on me," Harrison wrote to a friend. In desperation, he began contemplating a scheme for leading an expedition of volunteers to the "frontiers of Mexico"—the place that is now Texas. "My constitution seems suited to exposure and hardship," he wrote optimistically. But Harrison was now past sixty and about to be leveled by fever and ague.

In 1836, Harrison was rescued again by a government job when he was appointed clerk of the county courts. The job carried no salary, but the fees amounted to as much as ten thousand dollars per year. It was a lifesaver, or at least an estate saver. Harrison plunged himself in the work, with the help of his son Carter, who was studying law. A French traveler, passing through Cincinnati, recalled seeing "a man of about medium height, stout and muscular, and of about the age of sixty years yet with the active step and lively air of youth." A friend told him that it was "General Harrison, clerk of the Cincinnati court of common pleas. . . . He is now poor, with a numerous family, neglected by the federal government."

Harrison seemed to have come to the end of his public life. He had lost a bid for the U.S. Senate in 1831 and had discovered that there was not enough enthusiasm among his friends to mount another run for Congress. His county clerkship kept the financial wolves at bay, but he was in perpetual money difficulties. He was also unwell, suffering from ague. Always cheerful, he soldiered on. But he must have felt that his career had ended on a rather low note.

Yet he was about to become a candidate for president of the United States, an office he would win four years later.

6

The First Campaign

Andrew Jackson's presidency had been so strong that it had created two political parties—Jackson's Democrats and the Whigs, whose unifying principle was simply opposition to Old Hickory and all his works. For every political appointment Jackson had made over almost eight long years in office, he had probably created ten disappointed enemies. When Jackson vetoed federal support for a part of the great Cumberland Road system, he helped Henry Clay organize around support for roads and other "internal improvements." As Jackson declared war on the Bank of the United States, he added the bank's supporters to his restive opponents.

If the Whigs stood for anything more specific than anti-Jacksonianism, it was Clay's philosophy of a strong federal government where power was centered in Congress, not the president, and national policies encouraged economic development through public schools, a sound banking system, and the construction of roads and canals. But in reality the party's unity was mainly negative. There was a banking faction and an anti-banking faction. The Whigs appealed in the North to voters with abolitionist sympathies, and in the South to states-rights slave owners. As the Whigs' influential newspaper the *National Intelligencer* admitted, the party wanted a candidate who would rally all of its potential members "and we desire what is impossible." Clay, who was now a powerful U.S. senator and who some regarded as the only possible unifying force in the Whig Party, was not particularly interested in running what he regarded as a nearly hopeless race. Besides, he was in mourning for Anne, the last of his six daughters, who had died in childbirth.

So for the 1836 election, which Jackson's vice president, Martin Van Buren, was almost universally expected to win, the party fell back on nominating regional candidates. In theory, such a strategy might deprive Van Buren of a majority of the electoral votes and force the election into Congress. In reality, only the most wildly optimistic Whig could have imagined that the strategy would work. But many hoped that popular regional candidates might help draw voters for the Whig congressional and state tickets. As a Virginia supporter wrote to Clay, controlling the state government was "an object of great importance and almost a compensation for the loss of our presidential candidate."

In the winter of 1834–35, state Whig gatherings began to float names, and it looked as though the northern candidate was going to be Massachusetts' favorite son, Senator Daniel Webster. In the South, the Whig candidate was Senator Hugh Lawson White of Tennessee. In Ohio, the party looked toward Supreme Court justice John McLean, but McLean seemed lukewarm to the idea. He was apparently willing to take the job if it was offered on a plate, but not to fight for the nomination against other contenders.

Meanwhile, in Cincinnati, some of Harrison's old friends began to circulate his name as a possible candidate. Writing to a friend early in 1835, the delighted Harrison reported that "some folks are silly enough to have formed a plan to make a President of the United States out of this *Clerk* and Clod Hopper!"

Harrison's advantages were his military record—Andrew Jackson had shown the politicians how well being a war hero worked in electoral battles—and his very obscurity, which had left people with only a vague idea of what his positions might be on the issues of the day. He seemed an acceptable alternative for many anti-Jackson voters in the North who disliked Webster, and for members of the party's influential Anti-Masonic wing, who couldn't abide Clay, a Mason. Southerners were reminded that the general was a son of Virginia. And everyone knew that one of the first things Andrew Jackson had done as president was to fire Harrison from his ministerial post in Colombia.

Clay, whose enthusiasm for Harrison had cooled considerably over the years, still supported him as the candidate most likely to unify the party. Many of the other leading Whigs came around to Harrison as the best fallback position in a year when they had little hope of success. Nicholas Biddle, the famous banker, described him as a candidate "of the past, not the future," and recommended that the former general go with his strengths. "Let him then rely entirely on the past," he advised. "Let him say not a single word about his principles or his creed, let him say nothing, promise nothing. Let no committee, no convention, no town meeting even extract from him a single word about what he thinks now or what he will do hereafter. Let the use of pen and ink be wholly forbidden as if he were a mad poet in Bedlam."

Harrison campaigned in the manner of the day, which mainly involved allowing himself to be feted at dinners, corresponding with his supporters, and issuing a public letter in which he embraced some of Clay's political principles, such as

"internal improvements"—federally subsidized road- and
canal-building projects—and gave at least lukewarm nods to
others, such as a new national bank. And of course he denounced
Jackson as a dictator.

Harrison also had to deal with the problem of Richard
Mentor Johnson, who had fought with him in the Battle of
the Thames and had later been so helpful in Congress when
Harrison was struggling with his late son's debts. Johnson, a
colorful populist who had aligned himself with the Jacksonians, was going to be Martin Van Buren's pick for vice president, and as Johnson's star rose his supporters' insistence that
he had personally killed Tecumseh became a clamor. A periodical called *American Mechanic* ran a biography of Johnson
that included a claim that Harrison had deliberately refrained
from mentioning Johnson's great deed of valor when he filed
his official report. In response, Harrison collected testimony
from his former aides-de-camp saying that the story about the
killing of Tecumseh had not surfaced until months later.

Johnson was chosen to be Van Buren's vice president almost
solely because of his romantic Indian-fighter past. He was everything the plump, urbane Van Buren was not—a man of the
West, and the kind of man of the West that other men of
the West liked to imagine themselves to be. He himself never
claimed to have killed Tecumseh, although he never made any
attempt to discourage other people from saying so—frequently.
(After he died, his tombstone showed the late hero on a rearing
horse, firing into the face of an Indian.) During the campaign
of 1836, a five-act play, *Tecumseh, or The Battle of the Thames*,
toured the country, portraying Johnson as the chief's slayer.
Some theaters boasted a special display of what were supposed
to be the clothes Tecumseh wore and the rifle Johnson used to
kill him.

As Harrison became more of a threat to the Democrats, Johnson's identity as the Tecumseh slayer became increasingly important. The Battle of Tippecanoe, which became the center of the Harrison legend, was supposed to be about putting down the threat of Tecumseh, which it clearly did not accomplish. And although Harrison had led the battle that finally did eliminate the chief, he was not the one who had plunged into a mass of armed and angry Indians, rifles blazing.

There never was a single Whig nominee in 1836. The various parties and factions chose their candidates in different ways, but one of the most spectacular gatherings occurred in Ohio, where a 3,275-pound ox was barbecued in the Columbus public square before the thousand-plus delegates retreated to a theater and nominated Harrison for president. The newly elevated contender then took a trip to Virginia to visit relatives, along a route that wound up being well dotted with receptions and dinners. He told a supporter that he did not want to give the impression that he was "traveling for the purposes of Electioneering," which most Americans still regarded as undignified for a presidential candidate. But, he said, he did want to "counteract the opinion, which has been industriously circulated, that *I was an old broken down feeble man.*" In his midsixties, Harrison was indeed an old man by the standards of the time—the average life expectancy for a white male was then around forty-five. But he deeply resented the imputation that he was decrepit, a chorus that would grow even louder when he again ran for president in 1840.

Although Webster remained in the race, Harrison became the party's actual northern candidate, and he did more than respectably, carrying the states of Delaware, Maryland, Kentucky, Vermont, New Jersey, Indiana, and Ohio. Webster won Massachusetts and White took Tennessee and Georgia. But Van Buren won the election.

7

And Tyler, Too

The Whig nomination in 1840 was going to be much more valuable than the one in 1836. That became obvious within a few weeks of Van Buren's swearing-in, when the country plunged into the Panic of 1837. It was one of America's worst financial catastrophes. Banks suspended payments and businesses shut their doors. Up and down the eastern seaboard, factories closed and workers failed to receive their wages. Those who did get paid saw their salaries drop by 30 to 50 percent.

After Van Buren reversed Jacksonian policies that had contracted the money supply, a modest recovery ensued. But then the economy turned south again, and by the time Van Buren's term began drawing to a close the Whigs were confident that they were about to win control of the government. "Our cause everywhere is making sure and certain progress," wrote Henry Clay. "My *particular* cause could hardly be improved."

Clay was intent that 1840 would be his year, but he was far from the only person plotting. "We must prepare for the next campaign and profit by the errors of the last," Charles Scott Todd wrote to Harrison in April 1837. Todd, an old friend and the editor of the *Cincinnati Republican*, had also become Harrison's de facto campaign manager.

Almost as soon as Van Buren was sworn in, various groups and conventions started passing resolutions in favor of Harrison running again in 1840. In July 1837, the Ohio Whigs convened and expressed their preference for Harrison, while approving plans for an elaborate statewide organization to promote party candidates and party discipline. In New York, Thurlow Weed, the editor and Whig Party organizer, watched the activity in Ohio with disapproval. He loved the part about party organization—that was his passion—but he was unhappy about the Harrison business. It was too early to start "jarring among ourselves about a candidate for President," he wrote, when "the entire energies of our party should be exerted to arrest and defeat the destructive measures of the administration." (To translate: Weed didn't want his New Yorkers distracted when he needed everyone to concentrate on taking control of the state government in the 1838 elections.)

But to be fair, Weed admitted, Harrison's friends were forced to start mobilizing because the backers of other candidates were already also hard at work. The Ohioans "must either see him jostled off the course or do as others had done."

At that point, Weed was just coming into his own as a political strategist. Soon he would be known as a man who helped give the Whigs the same kind of discipline and marketing savvy that another New Yorker, Martin Van Buren, had given to the Democrats.

The era of party organizers and party kingmakers had begun with Van Buren and the election of Andrew Jackson, but the Whigs caught up quickly. Among Harrison's champions, Representative Thaddeus Stevens of Pennsylvania was one of the most important. Acid tongued, cynical, and crippled by a clubfoot, he would later become a leader of the radical Republicans in Congress, hated by the South during the Reconstruction era. But he got his start in the Anti-Masonic Movement of the 1830s. Stevens, a canny but perpetually angry man, once lashed out at the Masonic order as a "prostituted harlot" whose members, he claimed, drank wine out of human skulls. His opponents, in return, charged that Stevens had committed blasphemy by giving communion to a dog. It was that kind of era.

The Anti-Masons held considerable sway among the Whigs in some states, particularly Pennsylvania, and Stevens organized an Anti-Masonic convention outside Philadelphia where representatives from five states nominated Harrison for president and Daniel Webster for vice president. Clay denounced the "pretended convention," but Stevens simply moved on to promoting a state party convention in Pennsylvania that also passed resolutions praising the candidacy of Harrison–Webster. Clay's supporters organized a counterconvention that backed the Kentuckian.

In New York, Weed kept his own confidence and made favorable overtures toward both the Clay and Harrison forces. But behind the scenes he was moving to head off Clay, convinced that abolitionist sentiments in New York would make the Kentucky slave owner a losing proposition in the state. Meanwhile, Weed had glommed on to yet another possible candidate in General Winfield Scott, who had been extremely helpful to New Yorkers in the complicated "Caroline" affair, which involved an attempt to seize a Canadian island by a band of New York would-be revolutionaries, an imperiled steamboat, and a great deal of confusion. At fifty-four, Scott was the youngest of the potential Whig presidential nominees, and upstate New Yorkers became enamored of this newer, fresher version of the military hero as candidate. But they had no illusions that, outside of age, he was any different from Harrison. "The General's lips must be hermetically sealed and our shouts and hurras must be loud and long," advised a western New Yorker.

Clay was perhaps overconfident, and he certainly tended to underestimate Harrison's popular appeal. His early attachment to the general had cooled, and he was now telling his friends that Harrison was vain, shallow, and small-minded. Much of that new attitude must have stemmed from the change in Harrison's status—from a rather elderly protégé to a competitor. But it was certainly true that if judged against the example of Clay or Webster, the great statesmen of the age, Harrison's brief sojourns in Congress and his somewhat disastrous pass through diplomacy did not look particularly impressive.

The Whigs now had two preeminent statesmen and a pair of famous generals to choose from. To resolve the issue, the Harrison forces proposed a nominating convention—not a convention like the Democrats had, to ratify a predetermined choice, but one where the actual decision would be made about who would be the Whig Party's nominee. By the time Clay realized that this plan was greatly to his disadvantage, it was too late.

As the jostling for the nomination continued, Harrison nailed down the support of the Anti-Masons and a wide backing among the nation's large population of veterans, who remembered not only his war record but also his long-standing devotion to needy ex-servicemen and their families. He wrote to Clay, his old champion, expressing his chagrin—although a rather serene version of chagrin—at being in competition with the man who had done him so many services when he was attempting to win a place as a leading general in the War of 1812. "A few years ago I could not have believed in the possibility of my being placed in a position of apparent rivalry to you," he wrote Clay. "Particularly in relation to the presidency, an office which I never dreamed of attaining and which I had ardently desired to see you occupy. I confess I did covet the *second* but never the first office in the gift of my fellow citizens. Fate as Bonaparte would say, has placed me where I am and I wait the result which time will determine with as little anxiety as any one ever felt, so situated."

Clay believed with all his heart that he was the best man for the presidency. He had been working to achieve it for years, and the news that the old general, his ex-beneficiary, was calmly waiting to see if Fate would dump the prize in his lap must have been one of the most irritating letters he received in his life. Clay was a great leader in Congress—the place where the Whigs all agreed the major decisions of government should be made. And he had built the Whig Party around his own convictions about the importance of the federal government's role in growing the economy, in everything from road building to authorizing a national bank to manage the currency.

But those advantages were also his biggest problem. Although Clay tried to smooth the edges off his record, he had been a leader in the making of national policy for so long that it was hard to present his positions as anything other than what they were. On slavery, his actual worldview was not much different from Harrison's—both men said they disliked the institution but felt strongly that it could not be abolished without the approval of the states where it still existed, and both had talked about establishing colonies for ex-slaves in Africa and gradually easing the American population of blacks there. But Harrison had made his big decisions about the issue in the obscurity of Indiana Territory politics, or as a little-noticed backbencher in Congress. Clay had been a central player in all the great federal debates about extension of slavery into the territories, carpentering out compromises that wound up satisfying neither side. He also aroused the special enmity of the abolitionists because he was still a slave owner.

Many Whigs found it easier just to go with the military hero. Abraham Lincoln, a young Whig from Illinois, gave up on Clay and came out for Harrison. "So long as human nature remains as it is—so long as men continue ambitious of distinction—it is not the part of wisdom in any community to let that ambition go ungratified in an individual who has rendered arduous and valuable services," he wrote. It was certainly a convoluted road to an endorsement. Lincoln argued that if men like Harrison were not rewarded for their efforts, the nation's supply of future soldiers might be endangered. Who, he asked, would "care to sacrifice his ease and comfort, and spend all the better part of his life in bearing the burdens and encountering the dangers of his country if he shall know, that when he shall assert his claims to the gratitude of his country another, who has toiled not, shall be preferred to him?" Perhaps going overboard in stressing Harrison's advanced age, Lincoln concluded: "When an individual's hairs have grown grey and his eyes dim in the service of his country, it seems to us, if his countrymen are wise, and polite, they will reward him, as to encourage the youth of that country to follow his example."

Harrison did everything possible to press his advantage as a relatively blank slate. In a message to the Whigs in the New York state legislature, who had sent him a letter of support, Harrison expressed his opposition to the strong-president theory of government. His respect for the primary role of Congress was so great, he wrote, that he "declined, therefore, to give any further pledge or opinions on the subjects which belong to the future legislation of Congress."

Harrison was moving into this dramatic new stage of his life at a time of great personal pain. He and Anna had always been fortunate in their children's health—nine of their ten babies had grown safely to adulthood. Since then, they had lost two—Lucy, their second daughter, had died in 1826 at age twenty-six after bearing four children and John Cleves had succumbed to cholera in 1830 after fathering six. Still, at the time Harrison first ran for president in 1836, he and Anna could count themselves lucky in having seven surviving off-spring along with flocks of grandchildren.

But the years in which Harrison was campaigning for the 1840 nomination were filled with sorrow. In 1838 William Henry Jr. died at age thirty-five, a loss that was perhaps not unexpected given his years of alcoholism. Then the next year Carter, the lawyer who had helped his father with his work at the county court, died at age twenty-seven. And while Harrison was campaigning in 1840, Benjamin—the son who had become the physician his father never wanted to be—died at thirty-three, leaving behind a wife and infant daughter. William Henry stayed at home for a month to care for Anna, who had fallen ill after Benjamin's death. As much as the grieving parents might want quiet, however, a local paper reported that their solitude was interrupted by "numerous visitors."

· · ·

The Whig nominating convention was held in an old church in Harrisburg, Pennsylvania, beginning on December 4, 1839. It was the party's first convention ever, with local meetings called to choose the delegates. In a sign of things to come, "reporters of the newspaper press" were offered prime seats on the floor. Managing the press was one of the many skills the Whig organizers were mastering. It was perhaps an easier task than it is today, since newspapermen made no attempt to pretend they were not partisans—many hoped their journalistic efforts would win them a government job or printing contract. But the papers were important in a country where voters were spread far apart. Americans of Harrison's era had access to a relatively wide range of publications. One Massachusetts minister who began his adult life at the end of the eighteenth century remembered that back then his parishioners could only get their hands on a few copies of one weekly paper published in the region. But by the middle of the nineteenth century, he said, people could subscribe by mail to "342 newspapers, weeklies and dailies under fifty different titles—together with 55 other periodicals every month."

With Weed maneuvering behind the scenes, the delegates adopted a complex set of convention rules that boiled down to winner-take-all for the convention votes of each state. Clay had strong minority support in New York and a number of Harrison's states, such as Pennsylvania and Ohio, but he did not have the majority, and so it would count for nothing.

On the first ballot, Clay led with 103 votes, while Harrison had 91 and Scott 57. But then Clay's support faded as the more skillful operatives of the two generals went to work on his delegates. By the second ballot Scott seemed to be on the ascendancy. Then Thaddeus Stevens made his way to the Virginia delegation. Walking through the crowd of delegates, he casually dropped a piece of paper in a place where it was bound to be picked up and read. It was a letter from Scott to some New York abolitionists, expressing support for their cause. The Virginians quickly announced they would under no circumstances back Scott, and the momentum shifted to Harrison. Weed, seeing the tide, threw his support behind the Ohio general and, on the third ballot, Harrison won the nomination with 148 votes.

The Whigs immediately published their first campaign pamphlet, reproducing a convention speech by Judge Jacob Burnet of Cincinnati, a friend of the general's. With Harrison, Burnet promised, the Whigs would campaign "to save the liberty, the morals and the happiness of the people and to rescue the constitution from the hands of profligate men, under whose management it is sinking into decay." He also told a story—the kind of tale that would multiply like rabbits over the ensuing months—about a minister who dropped by Harrison's "log cabin" during a long and arduous trip. After receiving a good dinner and a night of gracious hospitality, the minister discovered the next morning that his exhausted steed had dropped dead. The general then insisted on giving him one of his own horses, Burnet said, and the minister went on his way, "his heart overflowing with gratitude and his prayers directed to heaven for blessings on the venerable hero." Except for the log cabin angle, it was one of the few Harrison campaign sagas that actually seemed conceivable.

After the delegates had celebrated their nominee, the next challenge was to fill the bottom of the ticket. The Whig king-makers hoped to find someone who would soothe the unhappy Clay supporters in the South, but the serious Clay men were bitterly disappointed and none was willing to run. Weed judged the situation as "anything but cordial" and the Harrison forces may have been a bit desperate by the time they landed on a Virginian, Senator John Tyler.

Weed had originally hoped to set up the vice presidential

nomination with as much care as the top of the ticket. In the spring of 1839, he had gone to Washington and called on Daniel Webster. The two men met in the Capitol cloakroom, and when Webster expressed hope that he would be the presidential nominee, Weed told the great Massachusetts lawmaker, "It looks to me like Harrison." When Webster started listing all the ways in which he was Harrison's superior as a politician and statesman, Weed responded calmly: "The question is—who will poll the most votes." He urged Webster to consider the second slot, but Webster categorically refused. It was one of those moments when you can imagine an alternative path into the future closing itself off.

Webster and virtually everyone else who might have been a first choice rejected a post that had traditionally been regarded as meaningless at best. The vice president had so little to do that the men who occupied the job often never even bothered to come to Washington during their term of office. Van Buren had been different, but his bond with Jackson had been forged long before. And having made it through eight presidencies without any serious health crises, people had stopped seriously contemplating what would happen if Number Two suddenly became Number One.

So the ticket makers turned to Tyler. He was one of those Whigs whose connection to the party seemed to begin and end with opposition to Jackson. He did not believe in a strong federal government—in fact, he was an ardent states-rights man. He opposed federal road-building projects not only on constitutional grounds but also because he regarded it as a form of charity that it would insult proud Virginians to accept from Washington. He had been nominated for vice president in 1836 by the Whigs in several southern states but had stayed home and made no efforts to further the ticket's prospects.

Tyler and Clay had worked together in the Senate, and although Clay was rumored to have tried to increase his own support in Virginia by backing an opponent for Tyler's Senate seat, Tyler had gone to the convention as a Clay delegate. When Clay lost the nomination, some delegates claimed to have seen Tyler weeping, although Tyler himself said it wasn't so. But the rumor may have helped the Harrison organizers settle on the Virginian for second place.

Tyler—who was from the same county in Virginia where the Harrisons' Berkeley plantation was located—acknowledged later that he had kept completely silent about his own beliefs when the negotiations over the vice presidency were under way. There were certainly many other Whigs whose ties to the party were as ideologically tenuous. But of course none of them were being nominated to be vice president on a ticket with a sixty-seven-year-old presidential candidate. Nobody seemed to think about it. In fact, no one took the trouble to quiz Tyler about his beliefs then, or at any other time until after Harrison's sudden death.

"Tyler was finally taken because we could get nobody else to accept," said Weed. As the crowds yelled for "Tippecanoe and Tyler, too!" the New York diarist Philip Hone concluded that the ticket had "rhyme but no reason to it."

None of the candidates was present for the voting, and when Clay heard the results he was undoubtedly crushed. One much-told story had him drunkenly complaining that he was "the most unfortunate man in the history of parties" who was always delegated to run when he was sure to be defeated "and now betrayed for a nomination when I, or anyone, would be sure of an election." The story is not reliable, although certainly Clay's supporters, knowing that he had been given the unenviable job of running against Andrew Jackson in 1832, when the popular president was seeking a second term, might well have presumed that this was what their hero was feeling. The only thing that is certain is that Clay rallied behind the party's choice, and sent word to Harrisburg urging the delegates to make the vote for Harrison and Tyler unanimous. At a testimonial for the Kentucky senator, Clay warned his unhappy southern backers to get in line. "We have not been contending for Henry Clay, for Daniel Webster or for Winfield Scott. No! We have been contending for principles. Not men, but principles are our rules of action." As time went on, he would decide that while he would not be running the country as president in 1841, he could probably run it through Harrison, and he campaigned vigorously for the ticket.

The Whigs had no platform—the Democrats would adopt one, perhaps to showcase the fact that the Whigs didn't. The party was certainly all over the map, encompassing southern slave owners, northern abolitionists, pro- and anti-tariff factions, and many variations on theories about a national bank. But the practice of having platforms was not yet an established tradition and few voters felt cheated for the lack. (Once the platforms became routine, of course, no one consulted them anyway.) But voters who wanted to know where each party stood had plenty of reason to assume that the Whigs were in favor of a strong federal government that would help develop the national economy, a public school system—something Harrison had actually advocated himself in Ohio—and a president who was far more deferential to the wishes of Congress than Andrew Jackson had been. The Democrats, when they gathered in Baltimore in May 1840, officially declared themselves opposed to federal assumption of state debts, a national bank, or those federal road- and canal-building projects many Whigs seemed to love so much.

Experts would later see the election of 1840 as a war between those who believed in a market economy and those who feared it. Or between the nativist Protestants the Whigs represented and those who were less threatened by the growing melting-pot complexion of the country. For the majority of voters, though, the campaign probably boiled down to variations on the promise that the Ohio gubernatorial candidate Tom Corwin made to America's farmers—wheat would be forty cents a bushel if Van Buren were reelected but a dollar a bushel if the voters chose Harrison. Times were bad, and this was a chance to throw the insiders out.

8

Log Cabin and Hard Cider

In February 1840, the Ohio Whigs held their state convention to celebrate the nomination of William Henry Harrison. "It was an army with banners moving through the streets whose walls were hung with flags, streamers and decorations in honor of a brave old patriot and pioneer, who had given the best strength and years of his life to protecting the poor men and women and children in the frontiers," said a Whig newspaperman, Anthony Banning Norton. He continued, without drawing a breath or starting a new sentence: ". . . and who had settled down in a log cabin to spend his days as a humble farmer at North Bend; and when the people had called upon him in his retiracy to serve them, had been vilified, slandered and traduced by the office-holders and a pensioned press."

The parade was spectacular, Norton reported. "Yonder comes a real, *bona fide* log cabin! See the raccoon skins hanging out upon its sides. Upon the door is written with charcoal, in awkward characters, 'Hard Cider.' It is filled with men in hunting shirts, eating corn-bread and as many of the same description as can sit on the roof or hang upon it in any way, are singing rude songs in praise of the 'Log Cabin Candidate.'"

The story of how the Democrats sneered at Harrison as a pensioned-off nobody and how the Whigs, in response, created the Log Cabin candidate is one of the most famous sagas in the history of ridiculous presidential campaigns. "Give him a barrel of hard cider and a pension of two thousand a year on him and, our word for it, he will sit the remainder of his days in a log cabin by the side of a 'sea coal' fire and study moral philosophy," jibed a Democratic paper, the *Baltimore Republican*. (Sea coal is very cheap fuel.) The Whigs could not have had a more perfect jumping-off point for a campaign. They quickly turned the log cabin and hard cider into a metaphor for Harrison's sturdy frontier virtues. It also became a homily about insiders and outsiders: Van Buren, the power-hungry Washington manipulator who liked to live high and wear fancy clothes, versus Harrison, the humble servant of his country who wanted nothing more than to rest from his long labors but was ready to answer the call to duty. Even today, when candidates employ armies of consultants to figure out how to get the advantage of an opponent, it would be hard to think of a stroke of marketing genius to match this one.

"Let Van from his coolers of silver drink wine," the Whig crowds sang,

> And lounge on his cushioned settee.
> Our man on a buckeye bench can recline,
> Content with hard cider is he.

"Van Buren had been brought up in affluence and had lived in luxury and had spent his days, as a lawyer and politician, in the fashionable circle, while Harrison had been from youth on the frontier, a soldier enduring hardship and privation," Norton told his readers. Of course, in the real world, Harrison was the one brought up on a Virginia plantation with tutors to see to his education, while Van Buren was the son of a not-terribly-successful tavern owner and grew up speaking Dutch, with no schooling except whatever he procured for himself. But the Whig spin was so successful, or so irrational, that party propagandists could extol Harrison's humble roots in one breath and then brag about his lineage as the son of The Signer in the next.

The new world of political campaigning had begun with Andrew Jackson and the popular vote, when the power to elect a president spread beyond the propertied elite. The revolution was abetted by cheaper postal service and a plethora of penny newspapers obsessed with politics. Van Buren, Jackson's strategist, had shown how it could all be put together in a national campaign organization that would stick to the messages sent down from the central leadership. The voters were encouraged to embrace a candidate's nickname ("Old Hickory") with symbols (old hickory sticks) and to feel patriotic and virtuous while treating themselves to parades, picnics, and songs.

The average American voter in this new era lived on a farm, where he and his family worked incessantly, spending their nights in small, dimly lit houses in relative silence. There were no sports and few public entertainments. So the chance to sing, parade, or lift a flagpole for a presidential candidate was a marvelous diversion. People would happily turn out for almost anything that offered a break from their usual routine, even if it was just to cheer the arrival of an oversized ball being rolled from town to town in honor of their party's nominee. (The balls were generally made of paper and covered with political slogans. The Whigs in Cleveland constructed one of tin, twelve feet wide, and pushed it all the way to Columbus in Harrison's honor. Another ball, made of cowhide, was even larger and had to be pulled by a team of oxen. Naturally, the Whigs adopted a motto of "Keep the ball rolling.")

The Democrats had pioneered some of these same entertainments in Jackson's campaigns. Now, everything would reach a new level, "a revolution in the habits and manners of the people," complained John Quincy Adams. Only a short time before, elections had been matters for the elite property owners, elected officials, and other members of the insider class. They, too, expected entertainment with their politics, in the form of private dinners and balls where they could enjoy the company of people they already knew through previous business and political dealings. Now average Americans were at the center of the campaign, and they were wooed with ox roasts and pole raisings and parades. The Whigs' candidate, meanwhile, would become an almost imaginary figure, drowned under a sea of log cabins.

"Log-Cabin Meeting this Evening. Boys! Do You Hear That?" one placard proclaimed. "Glorious news will be communicated. The vocalist, Mr. J. Brown, recently arrived from a Southern Tour, will sing several celebrated, bang-up Tippecanoe Songs!" How could a farmer or laborer, facing a normal night in his quiet, cramped, and gloomy home, resist—especially since the affair would probably be lubricated with Harrison Hard Cider?

The Whigs held yet another convention in Baltimore in May, at the exact time and in the same city where the Democrats were having theirs. They opened with a monster parade— alleged to be three miles long—featuring a huge ball that had been rolled all the way from the frontiers of western Maryland and—according to at least one eyewitness—more than one thousand banners. The streets were crowded with log cabin floats and many variations on hard cider and Tippecanoe. (An early attempt to create a new version of "Old Hickory" by nicknaming Harrison "Old Buckeye" had already faded.) The crowd then repaired to the Canton Race Track, where they listened until dark as speakers crowbarred the symbols of the hour into every possible paragraph. ("We have fallen, gentlemen, upon hard times, and the remedy seems to be . . . HARD CIDER!") The president of the convention, John McMahon, announced that the Whigs were now a "Log-Cabin Party," and another speaker urged the "log cabins of the country" to demand a return to constitutional government.

The log cabin image grew to be so powerful that it became almost imperative for every Whig politician to find a log cabin in his history. Daniel Webster, who threw himself into the new order of things with fervor, admitted that while he himself had missed the much-desired opportunity to be born in such a humble home, his elder brothers and sisters were log cabin products. "That cabin I annually visit," he declaimed dramatically, "and thither I carry my children . . . and when I or they forget that cabin and what it teaches and recalls may my name and their names perish from among men forever!" Webster deposited the log cabin at the wrong end of Harrison's story, referring to him as "a man who, by his capacity and industry, has raised himself from a log cabin to eminent station." But that was understandable—even if the public loved the log cabin image, there was really no place in the American dream for a hero who started out in a mansion, worked hard, and ended his days in a rustic hovel. Webster might have bemoaned the fact that he was born too late to be delivered into the world in his family's log cabin, but he never expressed a wish that his current home could be one.

Campaigning for Harrison, Webster discarded his traditional grand manner of speaking for a more conversational style, and he sprinkled his itinerary with rural destinations that required camping out rather than hotel accommodations. That was the rule for all the Whigs—everybody was going *log cabin*. The party had more genteel aristocrats among its leadership than the Democrats, but few of them made it through the campaign without being remade into men of the people. Hugh Swinton Legaré of South Carolina, the former editor of the *Southern Review*, reported that he had been on a "slang-whanging expedition" through five states.

The campaign organizers called Harrison's home the Cabin, although of course they knew it was no longer any such thing. The family's current house was clapboard and very big, although it was really not all that fancy. Horace Mann, the Massachusetts educator, reported after a visit to North Bend that in the parlor and drawing room, some of the pictures on the walls had no frames and "the whole furniture and ornaments in these rooms might have cost $200 or $250." Since $250 in 1840 was the equivalent of more than $6,000 now, it would hardly be the decorating budget of an old soldier in a log cabin. But it was apparently much more modest than Mann had anticipated. One wonders what would have become of the Whig campaign if Harrison had remained in Grouseland after his term as governor had ended.

Harrison's supporters circulated stories about his generosity—how any old soldier would always find the door open to him—and these tales were mostly true. They also emphasized the simplicity of his lifestyle—how Daniel Webster, visiting the Harrison home, had asked for French wine with his dinner and was told by his host that he couldn't afford such regal fare, but that there was hard cider at the ready. Those accounts were mainly fiction.

While Harrison was depicted as the humble soldier, the Whigs portrayed Van Buren as a dandified fop, living high while the people suffered. It was the combination that made their campaign theme work so well. One of the most circulated diatribes of the campaign was a speech by Representative Charles Ogle of Pennsylvania titled: "The Regal Splendor of the Presidential Palace." In hard times politicians always try to brand their opponents as big spenders, but Ogle's oration was in a class by itself. The speech, which took three days to deliver on the floor of the House, portrayed Van Buren eating fancy French meals off gold plates and admiring himself in gold-framed mirrors. The White House lawn, Ogle declaimed, had been landscaped with mounds "every pair of which was designed to resemble AN AMAZON'S BOSOM with a miniature knoll or hillock at its apex to denote the nipple."

No one cared that Van Buren's White House, which Ogle denounced as a "palace as splendid as that of the Caesars, and as richly adorned as the proudest Asiatic mansion," was in fact a dismal place full of worn-out furniture and peeling wallpaper. Everybody knew that Van Buren was something of a dandy who enjoyed good food. So the vision was cast.

"The cabinet assembled there," the Whigs sang,

> While thousands in each State
> Have not the wherewith to purchase food,
> They dine on golden plate.

The Whigs invented the political songbook, the better to create public entertainment under the guise of an exercise in citizenship. (Theirs, of course, was called *The Log Cabin Songbook*.) "A good club of singers and new songs and airs, made the air thrill with popular excitement," one Whig recalled. Horace Greeley wrote happily to Thurlow Weed, "People like the swing of the music. After a song or two they are more ready to listen to the orators." There was also a book of *Log Cabin Anecdotes* and a *Tippecanoe Text Book* for ambitious Whigs who wanted to have an argument for any Democratic claim. More popular, however, were the "Tippecanoe Quick-Step," which could be danced at a "Harrison Hoe-Down," not to mention the new Tippecanoe Shaving Soap, Tippecanoe Tobacco, and many variations on the theme of the Harrison and Tyler Necktie.

People gladly flocked to hear the great orators of the day speak on Harrison's behalf—even though, as John Quincy Adams noted, "not one in ten" could actually hear what was being said in an age of big crowds and no voice amplification. It was the excitement of the event, not the specific sentiments of the speaker, that mattered.

The ever energetic Whig organization had more than five thousand speakers out on the stump, by one reporter's estimation. Some of the most popular were the most plainspoken and entertaining, such as John Bear, "The Buckeye Blacksmith." Bear began his career at an Ohio convention that he attended as a plain local civilian. He was persuaded by his friends to make an impromptu speech that ended when he challenged an anti-Whig editor to a fistfight. His performance so delighted the crowd that he became a permanent touring speaker, mounting the stage dressed for work with his blacksmith's tongs, which he used to decimate copies of the opposition press, and an anvil and hammer, which he used to prove he was no "broken down lawyer."

The Buckeye Blacksmith was followed by "The Kinderhook Blacksmith," who shouted out what he claimed were neighborhood stories about his former fellow townsman Martin Van Buren. While they and other orator-blacksmiths faded away after the election, Henry Wilson, "The Natick Cobbler," used his career as populist speaker as a first step toward a political career that would end in the vice presidency under Ulysses S. Grant.

In New York, Horace Greeley began cranking out a campaign newspaper, *Log Cabin*, which would eventually have a circulation of more than eighty thousand. More than 90 percent of white Americans were literate, according to the 1840 census, and the Whigs were determined to take advantage of that fact. There was a raft of local *Log Cabin* periodicals, along with *Hard Cider Press* and a Cleveland publication called *Hard Cider for Log Cabins*. The Ohio Whigs alone published seventeen campaign sheets, one of which—having apparently run out of log cabin and cider titles—was named *Old Tip's Broom*.

In Philadelphia, a distiller named E. G. Booz created an election souvenir of whiskey in log cabin bottles, which helped popularize the word *booze* as a synonym for alcohol. (The roots of "booze" are complicated, and wind all the way back to fourteenth-century Dutch and Middle English. But the Harrison campaign seems to have made it part of the American lexicon. There's a similar story for "okay," which became part of the everyday American vocabulary courtesy of Martin Van Buren's nickname "Old Kinderhook.")

American elections had always been an excuse for drinking and carousing, but the Whigs went out of their way to encourage it, while also portraying themselves as the party of family values. ("Wherever you find a bitter, blasphemous Atheist and an enemy of Marriage, Morality and Social Order, there you may be certain of one vote for Van Buren," Greeley hyperventilated.) It was also ironic that Harrison, who had spent so much of his life trying to reduce drinking in the military, among Indians, and later by one of his own sons, was in the midst of a campaign that was based to a great degree on alcohol consumption. Hard cider, or fermented apple juice, could pack a serious kick. And at the inevitable banquets, the custom was to drink thirteen toasts in honor of the Founding Fathers, the Constitution, Tippecanoe, Tyler, too, and of course the log cabin. Harrison, when he was present, made sure not to appear unenthusiastic himself.

The log cabins that were raised in many towns to serve as centers for Whig activity were usually well stocked with hard cider. The *Washington Globe* described them as "groggeries" where depraved Harrisonians became "debauched with liquor." "Within three or four months, intemperance has become a badge of political party," decried a leader of the New York State Temperance Society. There were complaints in a number of cities about fighting and disturbing the peace. The brawling became so intense that John Quincy Adams claimed he was fearful of civil war.

"Hush-a-bye baby," the Democrats sang,

> Daddy's a Whig
> Before he comes home
> Hard cider he'll swig.
> Then he'll be Tipsy
> And over he'll fall,
> Down will come Daddy
> Tip, Tyler and all.

The urban world of 1840 America was a violent one and the excitement of a political campaign tended to cause endless brawls; each side accused the other of attacks. (It's possible that women did not mobilize to demand the vote earlier because they connected elections less with the patient march of democracy than with drunken fistfights.) A Whig in Pennsylvania described an outrage in Lancaster to a local paper: "Coming down East King from the place where we keep our big ball, we were met by the Van Buren men." The Democrats "threw stones and broke several holes into our ball," he continued, and then attacked some of the party when they repaired to a tavern for a few drinks, using "clubs, stones, pistols, etc." to beat and bruise "several of our most worthy citizens." In another incident in Baltimore, Whigs claimed that "a gang of half-grown boys" tried to break into one of their parades with "a stuffed figure representing General Harrison as a petticoat hero." When a local carpenter took umbrage and tried to stop them, a Whig paper said, the carpenter "received a blow over the head from a stick, which deprived him of life."

Of course, Whig partisans shouted "Tippecanoe and Tyler, too!" at every opportunity. It was strange that Harrison's name was always paired with what was probably the least impressive battle of his military career. Until then, his admirers called him the Hero of the Thames. But "Tippecanoe" came to represent not one minor fight against an outnumbered village in Indiana but all the Indian wars and the War of 1812 combined.

"When Martin was housed like a chattel," they sang,

> Opposed to the war as you know,
> Our hero was foremost in battle,
> And conquered at Tippecanoe.

Perhaps the Whigs also liked "Tippecanoe" because its glory did not have to be shared with Colonel Johnson, now Van Buren's vice president. When the Whigs yelled "Tippecanoe and Tyler, too!" Democrats were supposed to respond: "Rumpsey Dumpsey, Colonel Johnson shot Tecumsey."

By the end of the campaign, Johnson was known as "Old Rumpsey Dumpsey." It was not quite as inspiring as "Old Tippecanoe," but it was a better ending than his supporters might have feared. He barely survived renomination, since southern Democrats were in an uproar over his personal life. A bachelor, Johnson had lived openly for years with Julia Chinn, a slave with whom he had two daughters. Until her death in 1833, Chinn had run all of Johnson's business during his long absences from home. There were many southern politicians who had fathered children by slave women. (Mary Boykin Chesnut, a white plantation wife, wrote that every southern lady "tells you who is the father of all the Mulatto children in everybody's household, but those in her own she seems to think drop from the clouds—or pretends so to think.") But the gossip that shocked southerners was that the vice president loved his daughters and was actually rearing them as if they were white. The *Washington Globe*, in Johnson's defense, printed a testimonial from the girls' tutor who swore that while his students, Imogene and Adaline, were intelligent women of high character, "no attempt was made to impose them on society, and although they were well educated, they never entered a schoolhouse for that purpose." By 1840 Johnson had made things worse by living with a new mistress who was also mulatto.

Perhaps in retribution for all the gossip about Johnson and the long-standing rumors that Van Buren was the bastard son of the miscreant Aaron Burr, the Democrats spread rumors that Harrison had fathered children by various Indian women. The story most mentioned had him siring three sons by a Winnebago woman, whose offspring received annuities of "about $1,000 apiece." (There seemed to be fewer allegations involving sexual misconduct with slaves. But at the end of the century, a black woman in Atlanta, Madeline Harrison White, would tell her young son Walter that they were descended from a female slave named Dilsia, whose six children by William Henry were given to his brother to avoid political scandal. It seems an unlikely story given Harrison's early departure from the South, but White, who grew up to become the head of the NAACP, believed it was true.)

Whig partisans did not generally address such scandalous charges. But they spent a great deal of time denouncing the Democratic attempts to undermine Harrison's credentials as a war hero. Harrison had been called a "petticoat general," or coward, by his enemies since the War of 1812. It was a reference to the fact that Harrison had resigned his commission before the war was officially over, and to a story that during the war the women of Chillicothe, Ohio, had sent the soldiers shirts but gave the cowardly Harrison a petticoat. This was never a serious issue—Harrison was always, in fact, coolheaded and in the thick of every battle. Still, in one attempt to defend Harrison's honor, the Whigs produced a statement from what they claimed was "a relative of Tecumseh," expressing astonishment at the "petticoat" claims. "If the departed could rise again, they would say to the white man that General Harrison was a terror of the late tomahawkers," the alleged Native American wrote.

Women were urged to take part in the campaign in 1840—another first. Whigs passed around stories about young women who had made it clear they would not give their hand to any young man who failed to support Tippecanoe and Tyler, too. This would become a classic campaign tale throughout the nineteenth century, although no actual woman making such a pledge was ever identified.

The most common method for women to express political support was by preparing food for those stupendous Tippecanoe feasts—one rally in Chillicothe allegedly featured twenty thousand pounds of bread along with meat from seventy sheep and twenty-one steers. Women also occasionally sat decoratively on floats, waving to the crowd with handkerchiefs that of course had log cabins stamped on them. But some took a more active role. Lucy Kenney became one of the first American women to write a political pamphlet, on the Whigs' behalf. Others called their own meetings and a few made speeches—something that was unthinkable to most Americans of the era. A Miss Jane Field addressed the Fayette County Whigs in Illinois, telling the crowd, "When the war whoop on our prairies was the infant's lullaby, our mothers reposed in security for Harrison was their protector." In May, when a huge crowd assembled at the site of the Battle of Tippecanoe to celebrate Harrison's victory, a local paper described the multitude as "fifteen acres of men"—along with "6,000 females."

Some found the presence of women shocking. "This way of making politicians of their women is something new under the sun," said one Democrat disapprovingly. Richard Johnson, who was a peculiar person to be making arguments about social decorum, told a crowd he was "sorry to say that I have seen ladies too joining in . . . and wearing ribbons across their breasts with two names printed on them" while "ministers of the Gospel and men professing morals are not only looking on with indifference [but] are actually joining in to carry on their abominations."

When it came to organizing anyone—men, women, children—the Whigs were raising the bar to new heights. An executive committee in Washington was composed of members of Congress, each of whom contributed his mailing list to the presidential campaign. Every county had its own organization, which was supposed to hold rallies, establish Tippecanoe clubs, and publish campaign pamphlets and newspapers. Finally, the organizations were tasked with getting out the vote. "In this county we are polling the townships and thereby ascertaining the certain strength of our friends—dividing them into tens and giving each ten into the charge of a committee man, making him responsible for bringing his men to the polls & if at 4 P.M. of the day of Election any one two or three of his men should not appear, to take his horse & go for them," Samuel Purviance of Butler, Pennsylvania, wrote to Harrison.

Harrison was not the one doing the organizing—although Purviance was undoubtedly eager that the future president should be aware of his efforts. The work was being done to some extent by Clay, and even more by the new generation of political organizers like Weed, who were less interested in running the country than in creating, and running, the machine. For much of the year Harrison stayed in North Bend, entertaining an endless stream of guests, humble and great, and attempting to abide by his wife's rule against discussing politics on the Sabbath.

He complained continually about the burden of answering his mail, which, while heavy for the time, was minuscule by modern standards. (In interviews, Harrison claimed to be receiving up to twenty-four letters per day.) Much of it contained queries about his stands on the issues; even more dropped hints about possible jobs to come after victory. Most of the letters were passed on to campaign workers to answer. Many arrived with postage due, which the always-strapped candidate told a reporter was costing him nearly one hundred dollars per month.

Toward the end of the campaign, Harrison went out speech

making himself—another breakthrough that symbolized the
erasing of the barrier between common Americans and their
chief executive. Even Andrew Jackson had stayed at home
while his surrogates roamed the country giving speeches. Van
Buren followed that tradition, despite pleas from Richard
Johnson, who claimed to have told the president that "he ought
to go out among the voters as I intended doing." (Johnson himself was such an ardent campaigner that he was accused of
touching off a riot in Cleveland.) Harrison was expressing the
traditional sentiments as late as May, when he declined an
invitation to a Tippecanoe rally along the Wabash River, saying that he felt "it might be improper." But by June he was
hard on the campaign trail. "When was there ever before such
a spectacle," asked a Democratic paper in Cleveland, decrying
the idea of "a candidate for the Presidency, traversing the country . . . advocating his own claims for that high and responsible
station."

Harrison was sensitive to accusations that he was a faux candidate, with no opinions of his own, and incapable of speaking
or writing for himself.

"Another gourd for General Mum," the Democrats sang,

> Whose fame is like his fav'rite drum
> Which when most empty makes most noise
> Hauzza for General Mum, my boys.

At a big speech in Columbus, Harrison complained to the
crowd that the Democrats were saying "that I have not only
a committee of conscience-keepers, but that they put me in
a cage, fastened with iron bars, and kept me in that." He
then went on to explain that much of his mail was answered
by an assistant, who passed along Harrison's already-stated

positions on the issues. The general then pointed out once again that he was beset by an average of twenty-four letters per day.

While Harrison was definitely not a puppet, he was less well known than the men who had held the office in the past, and he was still not all that far away from his life as a county clerk and struggling farmer. So it was not surprising that people should wonder if he was his own man, and also not surprising that he should feel irritated by the charges. He was also wounded by claims that he was too old and feeble for the job of president—"a living mass of ruined matter," as one Democratic paper editorialized. The Whigs pooh-poohed the talk about mortality in public but worried themselves, in private. Webster predicted victory in November "If Genl Harrison lives."

Eventually, the Whigs asked Harrison's doctor to issue a public report on his fitness—another first that would, unfortunately, not become routine until late in the twentieth century. Harrison's doctor declared that he was surprised by the general's "vivacity and almost youthfulness of feelings . . . his intellect is unimpaired. Bodily vigor as good as that of most men his age. Subject to no disease but periodic headache."

Harrison's speech making was partly an attempt to further demonstrate his fitness. After his first major speech, a celebration of the battle of Fort Meigs in the War of 1812, he wrote to Webster that he was sure he had "silenced the calumnies as to my bodily infirmities." And of course the Whigs had a song for it:

> Though gray be his locks
> There's a fire in his eye
> That flashes in scorn
> When a foeman is nigh

Harrison wound up giving twenty-three speeches over four months. He never shone as an orator, but the length of his speeches—one to three hours—provided evidence that despite his age he was in robust health. He would also thrill the crowds by calling on old soldiers in the audience to come onstage, recalling moments when they had fought together in a long-ago campaign. Before his appearances he worked the crowd, shaking hands and demonstrating the gregarious good manners that put everyone at ease and made an excellent impression. He was ready, willing, and eager to stress his support for the Whig vision of a weak president, bowing to the will of Congress. He vowed repeatedly to serve only one term. And then he talked about the War of 1812.

John Tyler stayed in Virginia and tried to abide by the tradition that vice presidential candidates, like vice presidents, should be seen and not heard. He did agree to one late summer tour, in which he was questioned and heckled about his policies on touchy questions like tariffs and banks. "I am in favor of what General Harrison and Mr. Clay are in favor of," he said on more than one occasion.

Tyler might have been persuaded to come out and campaign by the fact that Richard Johnson was happily wandering the country on his own speaking tour. But Johnson was one of the very few colorful weapons in the Democrats' arsenal. Their presidential candidate lacked the kind of background that lent itself to mythmaking. Van Buren had spent all his life in politics, and his nickname "The Little Magician" was in tribute to his ability to craft backroom deals. It was not the sort of thing you could put on a float.

Harrison spoke extemporaneously, often recalling some previous visit to the town, sometimes pandering wildly. He denounced immigrants to audiences with nativist sympathies, then expressed solidarity with them in towns with large German or Irish populations. While trying to avoid any outright lies about his home, he dropped enough references to log cabins to give the strong impression that he and his wife were living in one. He told northerners that the suggestion he was in favor of slavery was "a vile slander" while to a southerner he bragged that he had "done and suffered more to support southern rights than any person north of the Mason & Dixon's line."

But he was hardly more elusive on the issues than other candidates. And when it came to slavery he had been fairly consistent throughout his public life—decrying the institution while insisting that the slave owners had the right to continue the regrettable practice. In 1833, Harrison had given a speech in which he suggested that—with the states' permission—it might be possible to use the federal surplus to buy southern slaves and relocate them in colonies outside the country. "By zealous prosecution of a plan formed upon that basis we might look forward to a day . . . when a North American sun would not look down on a slave," he proposed. None of this made any impression on the abolitionists, some of whom formed a separate anti-slavery ticket, the Liberty Party, which nominated James Birney of New York and Thomas Earle of Pennsylvania. It would not have any major impact on the election to come, receiving only 0.3 percent of the vote.

The Democrats, who were stuck defending an administration that was not particularly well loved to begin with, and now got the blame for a bad economy, spent most of the campaign on the negative. Amos Kendall, the Democratic campaign manager, had told the party faithful to "abandon the defense of Van Buren" and just stick to attacking the Whig nominee. Obliging, a Democratic newspaper in Philadelphia declaimed: "General Harrison was always a coward, always a foe to the people, always as rapacious as Verres [a corrupt Roman general] and as infamous as Arnold. We know not whether most to scorn his imbecility, to hate his principles or wonder at his impudent effrontery."

Since Harrison had so sparse a record in Congress, the Democrats inevitably looked at his war record. If the cowardice claim was bogus, there were more substantial weaknesses— such as that failure to fortify the camp at Tippecanoe. Andrew Jackson announced that he "never admired Gen. Harrison as a military man, or considered him as possessing the qualities which constitute the commander of an army."

But all that was quibbling so long after the fact. The Democrats had trouble making anything stick, particularly in the face of the remorseless Whig rapid response team.

Isaac Crary, a Democratic congressman from Michigan and a general in the militia, took to the floor of the House of Representatives during a debate over road construction to denounce Harrison as an inept military leader and the "greatest egotist that ever wrote the English language." The next day, a Whig from Ohio, Tom Corwin, decimated Crary as a peacetime general, marching in hot from the field to unsheathe his sword "and with an energy and remorseless fury he slices the watermelons that lie in heaps around him." Poor Crary was made merciless fun of as the "watermelon general," so much so that he lost his seat and acknowledged later that Corwin "killed me dead politically."

In the stories about the Log Cabin campaign, the voters generally are depicted as happy dupes who were played for suckers by cynical candidates who dodged all questions about the issues and diverted the dim-witted public with stories about log cabins and frequent swigs of hard cider. But although Harrison could be very, very vague, he was not much more so than many modern candidates. Voters could deduce from his history and his public comments that he believed in economic development, federal road projects, and public schools, and that although he would never celebrate slavery he would never do anything to restrict it either.

Moreover, then as now, the basic question of the campaign was whether the country was happy with the current administration. If not, people would be very receptive to calls for change.

"Farewell, dear Van," the Whigs sang at their meetings.

You're not our man;
To guide the ship
We'll try old Tip.

9

Thirty-One Days

Voting began on October 30, and shortly thereafter the Whigs learned they had carried Ohio. In the early hours of the morning, a crowd appeared at the home of Harrison's son-in-law, where the general had been staying, celebrating the local victory and demanding a speech. Harrison complied, while suggesting that victory celebrations might wait until more states posted their results. But it was a sign of things to come—in terms of both victory and demands on the general's energy. He had been campaigning in a way no presidential candidate ever had done before, and because this was an age without radio or television, the connection with the voters had to be made one-on-one, in those massive rallies and in dinners and speeches and endless handshaking. A younger man than Harrison would have been drained by it all, but the sixty-seven-year-old farmer seemed determined to prove he was not too old for any challenge.

The election continued until November 18 as each of the twenty-six states worked its own way through the process of selecting a president. Most had opened the ballot to all white men, but six required that voters be taxpayers, and four others restricted the franchise to property owners. In South Carolina, the state legislature still decided how the electoral votes were to be cast. Harrison won 234 electoral votes to 60 for Van Buren, a landslide that masked the narrowness of the popular vote, which Harrison won by only a little more than 145,000 of the 2.3 million votes cast. The Whigs also won control of the House and Senate.

All that was left was to debate whether voters had intuited the Whig vision and supported it, or were exercising their natural right to toss out the party in power when times were bad, or were simply seduced by the tomfoolery of the Whig campaign. Horace Greeley compared the analysis of the Jacksonians.

> *Blarney Before Election:* Dear People! Nobody but *us* can imagine how pure, patriotic, shrewd and sagacious you are. *You* can't be humbugged! You can't be misled! . . . You are always right as a book and nobody can gum you. In short, you are O.K.

> *Blarney After Election:* You miserable, despicable, know-nothing, good-for-nothing rascals. . . . Led away by Log Cabin fooleries! Gummed by coonskins! . . . Dead drunk on hard cider! Senseless, beastly, contemptible wretches! Go to the devil!

One thing the wild, carnival-like election demonstrated was that people really enjoyed voting when they were encouraged to identify with one party and regard the other as villain, when they got to take direct physical part in the campaigns through parades and pole raisings and cider-filled parties. The turnout was 80.2 percent—an astonishing increase from 58 percent in 1836. It was a leap that would never happen again in American politics. New voters constituted more than a third of the turnout, and the election was perhaps the last in which the parties focused on converting the newcomers rather than turning out the base and trying to tack on added support from the uncertain middle. Democrats as well as Whigs were moved by the excitement of the campaign—Van Buren received almost four hundred thousand more votes in 1840 than he had as the victor in 1836.

But some in the nation's capital wondered whether the stress of the campaign had ruined the health of a man who was, by the standards of the time, quite elderly. "I think the strength of his mind is unabated but his body is a good deal shattered," said Clay. John Quincy Adams wrote: "Harrison comes in upon a hurricane; God grant he may not go out upon a wreck."

Harrison went to North Bend to prepare for his presidency, but he found no peace at home, where an endless flood of job seekers were waiting to see him. "I understand they have come down upon General Harrison like a pack of famished wolves," wrote Representative Millard Fillmore of New York when word leaked out that Harrison had bolted from his home to take refuge in Kentucky.

The president-elect still lacked political cunning or he never would have imagined that he could flee to Kentucky and avoid seeing Henry Clay. But Clay ran him to ground, lassoed him, and took him off to Ashland, his estate. There, Harrison's easy manners smoothed over Clay's ruffled feathers, and the two men seemed to come to agreement, especially since Clay had no desire to leave the Senate for a job in Harrison's cabinet. He had a great hope, however, of being the behind-the-scenes power in a Harrison administration, particularly since Harrison had signed on so vigorously to the idea of Congress being the driving force in setting national policy. They parted on the best of terms, with Clay believing that some of his picks would be included in a Harrison cabinet.

William Henry Harrison arrived in Washington to huge crowds and a snowstorm on February 9, his sixty-eighth birthday. His trip had begun in Cincinnati, where he spent a night in a hotel that was surrounded by noisy celebrants who kept the whole traveling party awake. He insisted on walking through the muddy streets to his riverboat, where he addressed the crowd from the deck, recalling with some emotion that when he had first docked at that spot he was a young soldier and the shore was covered with "dense and dark forest."

"Perhaps this is the last time I may have the pleasure of speaking to you on earth or seeing you," he told his neighbors presciently. "I bid you farewell. If forever, fare thee well." Anna, who had said that she wished "that my husband's friends had left him . . . happy and contented in retirement," stayed behind in Ohio, organizing the family affairs and recovering from her illness and bereavement. She was planning to arrive in Washington in the spring. Meanwhile Harrison's niece Jane Findlay and his son's widow Mrs. William Harrison were prepared to serve as White House hostesses.

The boat docked for receptions along the Ohio River, where Harrison shook hands, occasionally resting his weary right hand by switching to the left. In between there were crowds along the bank, waving and hoping to see the hero of the moment, who seldom disappointed. The steamer docked in Pittsburgh, where the huge crowd made it difficult for Harrison to make his way to the hotel, which would again be surrounded all night by well-wishers who managed to keep all the inhabitants awake. He then began the land trip to Washington, where the residents of every village and town on the route turned out to cheer him on. Harrison's days were a series of jolting rides that required incessant waving, interspersed by receptions, hand-shaking, dinners, toasts, and meeting with a constant stream of visitors. When he reached Washington he was greeted by bad weather and "a rolling sea of umbrellas," according to the *Log Cabin*. There was, of course, a log cabin ball, lit by 1,800 candles.

The National Hotel, where Harrison stayed, was so crowded the dining room had to be turned into a dormitory, while a shed was erected in the backyard to accommodate endless banquets, with hundreds of guests and toasts. The overcrowded hotel, the diarist Philip Hone wrote, was one long line of "cold galleries, never ceasing ringing of bells, negligent servants, small pillows and scanty supply of water." Harrison presumably got bigger pillows and more liquids, but he was also perpetually assaulted by guests and petitioners and requests.

After all the years of struggle, Harrison must have been thrilled by his great, unexpected success. "He talks and thinks with . . . much ease and vivacity," wrote Martin Van Buren, who had invited the president-elect to dinner in the White House. The outgoing chief executive was charmed and surprised: "He is as tickled with the Presidency as is a young woman with a new bonnet."

Not everyone was equally serene about Harrison's state of mind. Representative Henry Wise reported that although the president-elect seemed "elated" by the hubbub around him, he was suffering "a total derangement of his nervous system," as well as an arm so worn down that he was no longer capable of shaking hands.

Still, he did seem to be enjoying himself. Harrison walked around Washington without an escort, greeting passersby. Philip Hone was in Washington for the celebrations and recorded having seen, passing through the crowd on Pennsylvania Avenue, "an elderly gentleman dressed in black, and not remarkably well dressed, with a mild benignant countenance, a military air, but stooping a little, bowing to one, shaking hands with another, and cracking jokes with a third. And this man was William Henry Harrison . . . unattended and unconscious of the dignity of his position." Hone found Harrison's simplicity "a sublime moral spectacle."

Harrison even dropped in on the Senate, startling John C. Calhoun, who felt a tap on his shoulder and turned around to find himself facing the next president. As usual, Calhoun's reaction was gloomy. Harrison, he thought, did not look strong enough for the job that lay ahead.

The great, pressing challenge for Harrison was not slavery or banks or foreign affairs. It was job seekers. The Whigs had never before held national power, and every opponent of the Democrats, every enemy Andrew Jackson had made, every petitioner he had rejected, now looked to Washington with new hope. Anyone remotely connected to the incoming administration was deluged with requests. In New York, Horace Greeley complained he was "run down for letters, letters." John Chambers, one of Harrison's closest friends and aides, wrote that the endless horde of petitioners who marked him as a man with Harrison's ear and thus pursued him everywhere had convinced him that "the personal friend and confidant of a President was by no means so enviable a position as was generally supposed." Chambers turned down an offer of a cabinet appointment as secretary of the treasury but accepted instead the post of governor of the Iowa Territory. Harrison's closest campaign adviser, Charles Todd, seemed similarly converted to the idea that the best job in a Harrison administration was one as far away from Washington as possible. He sought and got an appointment as minister to Russia.

But of course the petitioners directed most of their hopes at Harrison himself, who was by nature and by history the last man capable of coldheartedly rejecting them. "His natural kindness of disposition was seen at every moment," wrote a traveler from Britain who was in Washington for the pre-inauguration weeks. "Whoever called to pay him a visit was sure to be asked to dinner, whoever called for a place was sure to get a promise; whoever hinted at a want of money was sure to receive a draft; until it became the common talk that the President was over-drawing his account, overpromising his partisans and overfeeding his friends."

The petitioners were not limited to the more humble office seekers who hung out at his doorstep, flooded his office with letters, and accosted Harrison personally every time he left his rooms. The movers and shakers of the Whig Party, each of whom felt he had been personally responsible for dragging Harrison over the finish line, had long lists of requests, demands, and expectations.

Clay listed the new president's positive qualities as "honesty, patriotism, a good education, some experience in public affairs and a lively sensibility to the good opinion of the virtuous and intelligent." It was a portrait of a perfect follower, someone who might perhaps look to Henry Clay for leadership. But Clay also worried that Harrison was given to "vanity and egotism." The president-elect seemed to be avoiding Clay whenever possible and bristling when the Kentucky senator pressed his ideas for cabinet appointments. We don't know if, as legend has it, Harrison actually rebuked Clay, saying: "You forget that I am president!" We do know he offered Clay the post of secretary of state, which the senator rejected, recommending Daniel Webster, who said yes. And that Clay wound up feeling completely rejected and out of the loop.

As always, every person made happy by an appointment was balanced by ten who were disappointed. The hugely desirable and profitable job of collector of the port of New York was sought by both Robert Witmore, a Clay applicant, and General Solomon Van Rensselaer, an old friend. However, they both lost out to a Webster nominee, Edward Curtis. Webster's influence over the new president may have been due to former representative Abbott Lawrence of Massachusetts, who had become a wealthy cotton-mill developer. Lawrence, who was one of Webster's patrons, had made the still-strapped Harrison a loan of five thousand dollars just before the inaugural.

Clay, at any rate, was furious, as was the Van Rensselaer faction. Many other people who had reason to expect a lot from Harrison were shocked when they got very little. Thaddeus Stevens, who may have given Harrison the nomination with his well-timed letter drop in the Virginia delegation, had hoped to be postmaster general but he was offered nothing.

• • •

On the great inauguration day, March 4, 1841, Harrison rode to the Capitol on his favorite horse, Whitey. He was followed by a parade of old soldiers and young supporters along with an endless train of log cabins. People said it was the greatest outpouring since the inauguration of George Washington. Harrison did not wear an overcoat, and he held his hat in his hand, waving it at the crowd. He had not forgotten the Democratic press calling him a "superannuated and pitiable dotard," and he was determined to demonstrate his virility—not to mention his learning.

Long ago, when he was governor of the Indiana Territory and his friend Thomas Worthington was elected as a U.S.

senator from Ohio, Harrison had written Worthington a letter of congratulations in which he also reminded him of the importance of not making long speeches. It was a lesson the old general had apparently forgotten. On that raw and rainy day, he spoke for nearly two hours—a record for an inaugural address that still stands—repeating his promise to serve for only one term, stressing the importance of states' rights. The speech dripped with the classical allusions Harrison loved. Webster, who had been permitted to read and edit it, told a friend that he had "killed seventeen Roman proconsuls as dead as smelts, every one of them." But others endured.

"Called from a retirement which I had supposed was to continue for the residue of my life to fill the chief executive office of this great and free nation, I appear before you, fellow-citizens, to take the oaths which the Constitution prescribes as a necessary qualification for the performance of its duties; and in obedience to a custom coeval with our Government and what I believe to be your expectations I proceed to present to you a summary of the principles which will govern me in the discharge of the duties which I shall be called upon to perform," Harrison began. The speech that followed was a worthy continuation of the one-hundred-word opening sentence. He moved directly into "a remark of a Roman consul."

Harrison's speech was not only very long, it was extremely vague. He devoted a great deal of time, for instance, to the presidential veto power—something Andrew Jackson had used far more than his predecessors. Jacksonian overreach had been a favorite topic of Harrison and the other Whig campaign orators, and once again on inauguration day Harrison explained at length how ill equipped he thought a president in Washington was to reject the consensus of a Congress representing the people in the many states. He then concluded that he believed the presidential veto should be used "only first, to protect the Constitution from violation; secondly, the people from the effects of hasty legislation where their will has probably been disregarded or not well understood and thirdly, to prevent the effects of combinations violative of the rights of minorities."

By the rights of minorities, he clearly meant slave owners rather than the slaves. But the list in toto seemed sufficient to cover just about anything. It's easy to imagine, if Harrison had lived, the president who promised to defer to Congress vetoing one piece of legislation after another because the bills were "hasty" or failed to properly understand the will of the people.

However, the speech has gone down in history solely because of its length, and its role in killing the speaker. Conventional wisdom holds that Harrison was left so exhausted and chilled by his oratorical effort that he contracted pneumonia. That seems as reasonable an explanation as any other for the illness that followed. But there were many contenders for the title of Fatal Blow. Harrison was always out in the elements during his early presidency. He walked around the city all the time, even doing his own shopping for food. The Reverend Cortlandt Van Rensselaer said he ran into Harrison at Washington's only bookstore, where the new president was buying a Bible, indignant that one was not a permanent part of the White House fixtures. On the day he was taken ill, he had walked through the rain and slush to tell a friend, Colonel John Tayloe, that he was to receive a diplomatic post.

Indoors, Harrison was perpetually exhausted and beaten down by the demands of job seekers and by internal fighting within his party. "Whether in his mansion or in his walks, in public or in private, under all circumstances and at all times, the office seekers still clustered around him," wrote Senator William Allen of Ohio. One visitor to the White House discovered Harrison trying to get to a cabinet meeting but blocked by a crowd of petitioners who refused to let him pass until he received their letters, documents, and requests. When Harrison agreed to comply, his pockets, hat, and arms were filled with papers, as were the arms of his attendant.

During his campaign Harrison had promised not to follow what the Whigs firmly believed had been a "spoils" system of filling all government posts with party favorites under Democratic regimes. And he did send orders to the federal departments that government employees should not be required to support the party in power. He also stood down members of his own party who were pressing him for a mass firing of Democrats to open the doors for still more Whig appointments. One congressman in attendance claimed that Harrison dramatically threatened to "resign before I can be guilty of such an iniquity." But of course we can have no idea of how intently he would have followed through, given the intense pressure he was under to provide jobs for the party faithful.

We have no idea how he would have done anything, but it's interesting to speculate how closely he would have adhered to his campaign promise that Congress, not the president, should be the principal force in setting government policy. His cabinet believed, following Whig prescription, that it was their job to lead the president, who would preside over their meetings but would be only one vote among the members when it came to final decisions. Harrison would have been a uniquely weak chief executive if he had gone along when his ideas collided with those of his appointees, and the early signs were that he was both too self-confident and too stubborn to comply.

He certainly did not seem to plan to let Henry Clay call

the shots, as Clay himself had presumed would happen. "You use the privilege of a friend to lecture me and I will take the same liberty with you—you are too impetuous," he wrote to Clay when the senator pressured him to call a special session of Congress to begin enacting Whig policies. Clay, heartbroken, believed that Harrison had banished him from the White House. He left town for Kentucky.

Perhaps Harrison was losing enthusiasm for the concept of the weak presidency. Or perhaps he had just lost enthusiasm for Henry Clay. At any rate, he ordered his secretary of the treasury, Thomas Ewing, to make sure the government anticipated enough revenues to keep it running until the legislature returned at the end of the year. When Ewing concluded that it could not, Harrison issued the order for a special session after all.

He would not live to see it convene. On March 26, a physician found him "slightly ailing," though still at work. By the next day, Harrison was reported "suddenly ill" with pneumonia, although the doctors deemed it "not dangerous."

He was then given the most thorough medical care available, which included bleeding and cupping, in which a hot cup was placed against the skin, creating blisters. There was also a regimen of pills, including laudanum, opium, castor oil, and camphor along with wine and brandy. Perhaps it was the care that killed him. At any rate, he suffered a relapse and died on April 4, after a month in office.

His last words were, like so much of what he had said during the campaign, opaque: "Sir, I wish you to understand the principles of the Government. I wish them carried out. I ask nothing more."

The country, which had never experienced the death of a president in office, was shocked. The voters had just voted for change, and now the presumed agent of change was gone. Comparisons to the death of George Washington, which Americans had been taught to regard as the greatest loss in national history, were everywhere. Even John Quincy Adams, who had complained so bitterly about Harrison's persistent job seeking and been so dismissive of his capabilities, was moved. Harrison, Adams wrote, was "amiable and benevolent. Sympathy for his suffering and his fate is the prevailing sentiment of his fellow citizens."

Harrison's body lay in state in the White House, in a coffin with a glass lid that allowed mourners to see the face of a president most of them had never actually gotten to know. On April 7, 1841, thousands of people lined the streets of Washington for Harrison's funeral procession. His horse Whitey trotted down the streets riderless, the traditional symbol of a fallen leader. Bells tolled, cannons were fired, and the parade of grieving dignitaries stretched for more than a mile. It was a blueprint for marking the untimely death of an American president that the country would continue to follow when Zachary Taylor and then Abraham Lincoln were lost, and ever after.

Anna Harrison, who never wanted her husband to run for president, was preparing to leave for Washington when word of William Henry's death reached the family. She stayed in North Bend, preparing a site for Harrison's final burial. The late president's remains were originally interred in Congressional Cemetery in Washington, and then transferred to a site near the grave of Anna's father, whose canny mixing of politics and commerce had produced title to most of the lands on which the Harrison family resided.

Anna had borne more children than any other first lady, but she would outlive all but one. Five of her six sons were already dead, and in the four years following William Henry's death, Anna lost all three of her remaining daughters.

Harrison's surviving child, John Scott, would be elected to the House of Representatives in 1853 and would serve until 1857, taking his father's middle road on most subjects, including slavery. John Scott also managed the family's land in North Bend, where he and his family lived in what was the most elegant of the homes on the Harrison lands—a colonial brick with a walnut grand staircase, whose hardware and glass had been carried to Ohio over the Allegheny Mountains.

Anna, who had always been interested in politics if not enthusiastic about her husband's involvement, kept close and disapproving track of William Henry's successor, John Tyler. But her main involvement in national affairs picked up on a theme of her husband's—lobbying important people in Washington to give jobs to her numerous grandsons and nephews.

In 1858, the fabled Big House/Log Cabin that had figured so centrally in American politics burned down. Anna moved in with John Scott's family, adding one more relative to a table that, like William Henry's, was crowded with nine children and other friends and relatives. Like his father, John Scott would struggle to balance his political duties with management of the farm and constant financial crises. However, his children were well fed and well educated. One son, bearing the magic name of Benjamin, would later become the only grandson of a president to be elected to the office himself.

Notes

PROLOGUE

3   "The house now so desolate a picture": George Elders, "Old Harrison House, Now Forlorn, May Become a Shrine," *Cincinnati Times-Star*, May 7, 1940.

1: TO THE MANOR BORN

10   Going upstairs to close a window: Anna Chieko Moore, *Benjamin Harrison, Centennial President* (Hauppauge, N.Y.: Nova Science, 2009), p. 6.

10   the British published an intercepted letter: Some scholars feel the entire Kate letter is a forgery. Others believe that only the George Washington part was false.

11   According to family legend: James Green, *William Henry Harrison* (Richmond, Va.: Garrett and Massie, 1941), p. 2.

11   "elegantly arrayed in a rich suit of blue and buff": Ibid., p. 4.

11   a "delicate" boy: Ibid., p. 10.

12   "the English grammar, Caesar's commentaries": Ibid., pp. 11–12.

12   "three times before I was seventeen years old": Ibid., p. 12.

12   In his diary, Pleasants had recorded: Stephen B. Weeks,

Southern Quakers and Slavery (Baltimore: Johns Hopkins Press, 1896), p. 212.

13   "had no reason to reject": Robert Owens, *Mr. Jefferson's Hammer* (Norman, Okla.: University of Oklahoma Press, 2007), p. 15.

14   "In 24 hours from the first conception": Freeman Cleaves, *Old Tippecanoe* (Newtown, Conn.: American Political Biography Press, 2000), p. 7.

14   the real impetus for Harrison's enlistment: Dorothy Goebel, *William Henry Harrison: A Political Biography* (Indianapolis: Indiana Library and Historical Department, 1926), p. 19.

15   The other officers were mainly veterans of the Revolution: Ibid., p. 28.

16   "At least four fifths of my brother officers": Cleaves, *Old Tippecanoe*, p. 10.

17   "a young gentleman of family, education and merit": Green, *William Henry Harrison*, p. 53.

2: THE GOVERNOR

19   "Such sums of money have been thrown away": Goebel, *William Henry Harrison*, pp. 28–29.

20   "dealt treacherously with us": John Sugden, *Blue Jacket, Warrior of the Shawnees* (Lincoln, Neb.: University of Nebraska Press, 2000), p. 179.

20   "there we could see Harrison giving the order": Cleaves, *Old Tippecanoe*, p. 21.

20   "General Wayne, I am afraid": Green, *William Henry Harrison*, p. 42.

21   "the fear of the Indians deters her": Ibid., p. 60.

21   "remarkably beautiful": Cleaves, *Old Tippecanoe*, p. 23.

22   "My sword is my means of support, sir!": Ibid., p. 25.

23   He had already sold the Tidewater land: Owens, *Mr. Jefferson's Hammer*, p. 39.

23 half the rich men in America: Norma Lois Peterson, *The Presidencies of William Henry Harrison and John Tyler* (Lawrence, Kan.: University of Kansas Press, 1989), p. 1.

24 But for its time it was substantial: Green, *William Henry Harrison*, pp. 407–8.

24 "My nursery grows faster than my strongbox": Cleaves, *Old Tippecanoe*, p. 55.

24 "I have been so long in these woods": Goebel, *William Henry Harrison*, pp. 39–40.

25 "His Excellency, the Governor": Green, *William Henry Harrison*, p. 71.

26 Later, in his presidential campaigns: Owens, *Mr. Jefferson's Hammer*, p. 50.

27 "460 French and about 40 American families": Green, *William Henry Harrison*, p. 92.

27 In a region full of humble wood-frame houses: Cleaves, *Old Tippecanoe*, pp. 44–45.

28 "one of the fairest portions of the globe": John Sugden, *Tecumseh: A Life* (New York: Henry Holt, 1998), p. 215.

28 "when I reflect on the unbounded thirst": Owens, *Mr. Jefferson's Hammer*, p. 8.

30 "because we observe that when these debts": Ibid., p. 76.

30 After one deal, in which a group of chiefs: Sugden, *Tecumseh*, pp. 106–7.

30 When Harrison offered them some food: Green, *William Henry Harrison*, p. 112.

30 "I wish I could say that the Indians were treated": Cleaves, *Old Tippecanoe*, p. 78.

31 "they make heavy complaints": Ibid., p. 34.

32 Harrison signed one treaty: Owens, *Mr. Jefferson's Hammer*, p. 80.

32 "pecuniary advances": Ibid., p. 100.

32 "Is there a man vain enough": Cleaves, *Old Tippecanoe*, p. 284.

33   "I have been the means of liberating many slaves": Owens, *Mr. Jefferson's Hammer*, p. 194.

33   "the reason for driving many valuable citizens": Green, *William Henry Harrison*, p. 104.

33   "under contract to serve another": Owens, *Mr. Jefferson's Hammer*, p. 70.

34   When one of his black indentured servants: Ibid., p. 240.

34   Harrison fought fiercely to protect George and Peggy: Ibid., pp. 72–73.

35   there be "no more Virginians": Ibid., p. 150.

3: TIPPECANOE

37   "Having spent seven years of my life": Owens, *Mr. Jefferson's Hammer*, p. 154.

37   "Perhaps one of the finest looking men I ever saw": Sugden, *Tecumseh*, p. 198.

37   "The implicit obedience and respect": Ibid., p. 215.

38   "Sell a country!": Ohio History Central, http:///www.ohio historycentral.org.

39   "some proofs . . . some miracles": Owens, *Mr. Jefferson's Hammer*, pp. 125–26.

39   "The story is that the Shawnee Prophet": Green, *William Henry Harrison*, p. 120.

40   "an engine set to work by the British": Sugden, *Tecumseh*, p. 158.

40   "Upon the whole Sir": Owens, *Mr. Jefferson's Hammer*, pp. 153–54.

41   "I know your warriors are brave": Sugden, *Tecumseh*, p. 197.

41   "the bosom of their mother": Ibid., p. 198.

41   "and for some minutes there was a perfect silence": Ibid.

42   "I do not see how we can remain": Ibid., p. 199.

42   "induce him to direct you": Sugden, *Tecumseh*, p. 202.

43   "My warriors are in motion": Ibid., pp. 226–27.

43   "Volunteers, show yourselves": Green, *William Henry Harrison*, pp. 119–20.

43   They were members of the Fourth Infantry Regiment: Ibid., p. 125.

43   "fixed with hooks and eyes": Ibid., p. 120.

44   "slender with sallow complexion": Cleaves, *Old Tippecanoe*, p. 89.

44   Harrison told them he understood their grievances: Ibid., p. 91.

45   "In common with the whole army": Goebel, *William Henry Harrison*, p. 121.

45   "Where is your captain?": Green, *William Henry Harrison*, p. 121.

47   "The Gov. Returned": Ibid., pp. 122–23.

4: THE WAR OF 1812

49   "the collected firmness which distinguished": Owens, *Mr. Jefferson's Hammer*, p. 222.

49   "The Blow Is Struck": Green, *William Henry Harrison*, p. 133.

49   "who does not know that the tomahawk": Owens, *Mr. Jefferson's Hammer*, p. xiv.

49   "The blood rises to my cheek": Ibid., p. 138.

50   "No military man in the U. States": Cleaves, *Old Tippecanoe*, p. 114.

50   "no immediate necessity": Goebel, *William Henry Harrison*, p. 134.

51   "in whose company we cannot": Ibid., p. 140.

51   As Clay admitted in a letter to James Monroe: David S. Heidler and Jeanne T. Heidler, *Henry Clay: The Essential American* (New York: Random House, 2010), p. 100.

52   Harrison guarded his supply lines: Owens, *Mr. Jefferson's Hammer*, pp. 223–24.

54   Word reached Washington, D.C.: Heidler and Heidler, *Henry Clay*, p. 104.

56   The Kentucky soldiers did find a body: Owens, *Mr. Jefferson's Hammer*, p. 229.

57   "He had come into the wilderness": Green, *William Henry Harrison*, pp. 209–10.

5: PURSUING A POST

59   "I am Settled here I believe for life": Owens, *Mr. Jefferson's Hammer*, p. 240.

60   The only actual hint of a log: Green, *William Henry Harrison*, p. 411.

60   "He kept an open table": Cleaves, *Old Tippecanoe*, pp. 230–31.

61   "handsome manners": Goebel, *William Henry Harrison*, p. 87.

62   "There was no speech making in this campaign": Green, *William Henry Harrison*, p. 226.

62   "You must spare no pains": Cleaves, *Old Tippecanoe*, p. 235.

62   "the whole secret of ancient military glory": Goebel, *William Henry Harrison*, pp. 215–16.

63   "The Western people are asked to pay": Green, *William Henry Harrison*, p. 229.

63   "to be feasted in the prytaneum": Cleaves, *Old Tippecanoe*, p. 243.

64   "is not known to be an enemy of banking": Green, *William Henry Harrison*, p. 236.

64   "the enemy of banks in general": Goebel, *William Henry Harrison*, p. 227.

64   Harrison won his election: Ibid.

65   "I have seen a great deal of human misery": Green, *William Henry Harrison*, p. 252.

66 "This person's thirst for lucrative office": Goebel, *William Henry Harrison*, p. 254.

66 "Harrison wants the mission to Colombia": Ibid., p. 255.

66 "My great object is to save a little money": Cleaves, *Old Tippecanoe*, p. 263.

67 "a simple and good man": Goebel, *William Henry Harrison*, p. 262.

67 "When a dinner is given": Green, *William Henry Harrison*, p. 268.

67 "If you had seen him as I did": Ibid., p. 275.

68 But only Harrison tried to split the difference: Goebel, *William Henry Harrison*, p. 222.

68 "Are you willing that your name should descend": Green, *William Henry Harrison*, p. 281.

69 "If you had not arrived here": Ibid., p. 283.

70 "Money is very scarce and hard to be got": Cleaves, *Old Tippecanoe*, p. 253.

70 "I will set myself to work": Ibid., p. 277.

71 "I have sold so much of my property": Ibid., p. 286.

71 "a man of about medium height": Ibid., p. 291.

6: THE FIRST CAMPAIGN

74 "and we desire what is impossible": Michael F. Holt, *The Rise and Fall of the American Whig Party* (New York: Oxford University Press, 1999), p. 39.

74 "an object of great importance": Ibid., p. 40.

74 "some folks are silly enough": Goebel, *William Henry Harrison*, p. 307.

75 "of the past, not the future": Green, *William Henry Harrison*, p. 295.

76 A periodical called *American Mechanic*: Cleaves, *Old Tippecanoe*, p. 288.

76   *Tecumseh, or The Battle of the Thames*: Sugden, *Tecumseh*, p. 397.

77   "traveling for the purposes of Electioneering": Cleaves, *Old Tippecanoe*, p. 305.

                          7: AND TYLER, TOO

78   "Our cause everywhere is making sure and certain progress": Peterson, *Presidencies*, p. 24.

78   "We must prepare for the next campaign": Goebel, *William Henry Harrison*, p. 325.

79   Thurlow Weed, the editor and Whig Party organizer: Thurlow Weed Barnes, *Life of Thurlow Weed* (Boston: Houghton Mifflin, 1884), pp. 56–57.

80   Stevens, a canny but perpetually angry man: Fawn Brodie, *Thaddeus Stevens, Scourge of the South* (New York: Norton, 1966), p. 41.

80   Clay denounced the "pretended convention": Goebel, *William Henry Harrison*, p. 333.

81   "The General's lips must be hermetically sealed": William Nisbet Chambers, "Election of 1840," in Arthur M. Schlesinger Jr., ed., *History of American Presidential Elections* (New York: Chelsea House, 1971), p. 660.

82   "A few years ago I could not have believed": Robert Gray Gunderson, *The Log-Cabin Campaign* (Westport, Conn.: Greenwood Press, 1977), p. 48.

83   "So long as human nature remains as it is": Chambers, "Election of 1840," p. 693.

84   "declined, therefore, to give any further pledge": Anthony Banning Norton, *The Great Revolution of 1840* (Mount Vernon, Ohio: A. B. Norton, 1888), p. 41.

84   "numerous visitors": Cleaves, *Old Tippecanoe*, p. 324.

85   In a sign of things to come: Chambers, "Election of 1840": p. 662.

85   "342 newspapers, weeklies and dailies under fifty different titles": Jack Larkin, *The Reshaping of Everyday Life* (New York: HarperPerennial, 1988), p. 54.

86   "to save the liberty, the morals and the happiness": Holt, *Rise and Fall*, p. 105.

86   "his heart overflowing with gratitude": Norton, *Great Revolution*, p. 37.

86   Weed judged the situation as "anything but cordial": Heidler and Heidler, *Henry Clay*, p. 309.

87   In the spring of 1839, he had gone to Washington: Barnes, *Life of Thurlow Weed*, p. 76.

88   "Tyler was finally taken": Peterson, *Presidencies*, p. 26.

88   As the crowds yelled for "Tippecanoe and Tyler, too!": Gunderson, *Log-Cabin Campaign*, p. 64.

88   "the most unfortunate man in the history of parties": Heidler and Heidler, *Henry Clay*, p. 310.

89   "We have not been contending for Henry Clay": Holt, *Rise and Fall*, p. 105.

8: LOG CABIN AND HARD CIDER

91   "It was an army with banners": Norton, *Great Revolution*, p. 49.

91   "Yonder comes a real, *bona fide* log cabin!": Ibid., p. 55.

92   "Give him a barrel of hard cider": Gunderson, *Log-Cabin Campaign*, p. 74.

92   "Let Van from his coolers of silver drink wine": Peterson, *Presidencies*, p. 29.

92   "Van Buren had been brought up in affluence": Norton, *Great Revolution*, p. 11.

94   "a revolution in the habits and manners of the people": Gunderson, *Log-Cabin Campaign*, p. 7.

94   "Log-Cabin Meeting this Evening": Goebel, *William Henry Harrison*, p. 353.

94   The streets were crowded with log cabin floats: Gunderson, *Log-Cabin Campaign*, pp. 4–5.

95   "That cabin I annually visit": Norton, *Great Revolution*, p. 11.

95   "a man who, by his capacity and industry": Ibid.

96   a "slangwhanging expedition": Gunderson, *Log-Cabin Campaign*, p. 199.

96   "the whole furniture and ornaments": Cleaves, *Old Tippecanoe*, p. 321.

97   "The Regal Splendor of the Presidential Palace": Gunderson, *Log-Cabin Campaign*, pp. 102–3.

97   "The cabinet assembled there": Norton, *Great Revolution*, "Tippecanoe Songs," p. 16.

97   "A good club of singers": Cleaves, *Old Tippecanoe*, p. 325.

97   "People like the swing of the music": Gunderson, *Log-Cabin Campaign*, p. 125.

98   "not one in ten" : Ibid., p. 115.

98   The ever energetic Whig organization: Chambers, "Election of 1840," p. 674.

98   Bear began his career: Gunderson, *Log-Cabin Campaign*, pp. 199–207.

99   "Wherever you find a bitter, blasphemous Atheist": Holt, *Rise and Fall*, p. 109.

100   The *Washington Globe* described them as "groggeries": Gunderson, *Log-Cabin Campaign*, p. 142.

100   "Hush-a-bye baby": Ibid., pp. 236–37.

101   "Coming down East King": Norton, *Great Revolution*, p. 370.

101   "a gang of half-grown boys": Ibid., p. 138.

101   "When Martin was housed like a chattel": Gunderson, *Log-Cabin Campaign*, p. 25.

102   "tells you who is the father of all the Mulatto children": C. Vann Woodward, *Mary Chesnut's Civil War* (New Haven, Conn.: Yale University Press, 1981), p. 29.

102   "no attempt was made to impose them on society": Gail Collins, *Scorpion Tongues: Gossip, Celebrity, and American Politics* (New York: Harcourt Brace, 1999), p. 54.

102   The story most mentioned had him siring three sons: Cleaves, *Old Tippecanoe*, p. 321.

103   a black woman in Atlanta, Madeline Harrison White: Kenneth Robert Janken, *White* (New York: The New Press, 2003), p. 3.

103   "If the departed could rise again": Norton, *Great Revolution*, p. 140.

104   Lucy Kenney became one of the first American women: Gunderson, *Log-Cabin Campaign*, p. 136.

104   "fifteen acres of men": Ibid., p. 118.

104   "This way of making politicians of their women": Ibid., pp. 245–46.

105   "In this county we are polling the townships": Goebel, *William Henry Harrison*, pp. 353–54.

105   up to twenty-four letters per day: Cleaves, *Old Tippecanoe*, p. 322.

105   Many arrived with postage due: Green, *William Henry Harrison*, p. 377.

106   "he ought to go out among the voters": Gunderson, *Log-Cabin Campaign*, p. 163.

106   he felt "it might be improper": Ibid., p. 164.

106   "When was there ever before such a spectacle": Ibid.

106   "Another gourd for General Mum": Chambers, "Election of 1840," p. 672.

106   "that I have not only a committee of conscience-keepers": Norton, *Great Revolution*, p. 169.

107   "a living mass of ruined matter": Collins, *Scorpion Tongues*, p. 47.

107   Webster predicted victory in November "If Genl Harrison lives": Peterson, *Presidencies*, p. 28.

107   "vivacity and almost youthfulness of feelings": Cleaves, *Old Tippecanoe*, p. 323.

107   "silenced the calumnies as to my bodily infirmities": Ibid., p. 326.

107   "Though gray be his locks": Norton, *Great Revolution*, "Tippecanoe Songs," p. 58.

108   "I am in favor of what General Harrison": Gunderson, *Log-Cabin Campaign*, p. 197.

109   He told northerners that the suggestion: Ibid., p. 225.

109   "By zealous prosecution of a plan": Cleaves, *Old Tippecanoe*, p. 284.

109   "abandon the defense of Van Buren": Gunderson, *Log-Cabin Campaign*, p. 228.

109   "General Harrison was always a coward": Green, *William Henry Harrison*, p. 346.

110   "never admired Gen. Harrison as a military man": Gunderson, *Log-Cabin Campaign*, p. 221.

110   Isaac Crary, a Democratic congressman from Michigan: Ibid., pp. 96–101.

111   "Farewell dear Van": Ibid., p. 4.

9: THIRTY-ONE DAYS

113   Horace Greeley compared the analysis of the Jacksonians: Chambers, "Election of 1840," p. 682.

114   "I think the strength of his mind is unabated": Heidler and Heidler, *Henry Clay*, p. 329.

114   "Harrison comes in upon a hurricane": Peterson, *Presidencies*, p. 31.

114   "I understand they have come down upon General Harrison": Gunderson, *Log-Cabin Campaign*, p. 259.

115   "Perhaps this is the last time": Cleaves, *Old Tippecanoe*, p. 331.

115   "that my husband's friends had left him": Ibid., p. 328.

116 "a rolling sea of umbrellas": Green, *William Henry Harrison*, p. 388.

116 one long line of "cold galleries, never ceasing ringing of bells": Ibid., pp. 389–90.

116 "He talks and thinks with . . . much ease and vivacity": Peterson, *Presidencies*, p. 33.

116 the president-elect seemed "elated" by the hubbub: Gunderson, *Log-Cabin Campaign*, pp. 262–63.

117 "an elderly gentleman dressed in black": Cleaves, *Old Tippecanoe*, p. 335.

117 "run down for letters, letters": Ibid., p. 334.

117 "the personal friend and confidant of a President": Green, *William Henry Harrison*, p. 381.

118 "His natural kindness of disposition": Goebel, *William Henry Harrison*, p. 377.

118 "honesty, patriotism, a good education": Heidler and Heidler, *Henry Clay*, p. 326.

119 Webster's influence over the new president: Cleaves, *Old Tippecanoe*, p. 339.

119 He had not forgotten the Democratic press: Ibid., p. 316.

119 Long ago, when he was governor of the Indiana Territory: Owens, *Mr. Jefferson's Hammer*, p. 70.

120 "killed seventeen Roman proconsuls": Goebel, *William Henry Harrison*, p. 373.

120 "Called from a retirement": Harrison's inaugural address is available online from a number of sites, including bartleby .com.

121 The Reverend Cortlandt Van Rensselaer said he ran into Harrison: Green, *William Henry Harrison*, p. 396.

121 On the day he was taken ill: Cleaves, *Old Tippecanoe*, p. 341.

121 "Whether in his mansion or in his walks": Green, *William Henry Harrison*, p. 395.

122 "resign before I can be guilty": Gary May, *John Tyler* (New York: Times Books, 2008), p. 60.

123   "You use the privilege of a friend": Heidler and Heidler, *Henry Clay*, p. 339.

123   "slightly ailing": Green, *William Henry Harrison*, p. 398.

123   He was then given the most thorough medical care: Ibid., pp. 398–99.

124   "amiable and benevolent": Peterson, *Presidencies*, p. 42.

Milestones

——————

1773	William Henry Harrison is born on February 9 in Virginia
1787	Enters Hampden-Sidney College
1790	Goes to Richmond to study medicine with Dr. Andrew Leiper
1791	Joins the army
1794	Fights in the Battle of Fallen Timbers under General Anthony Wayne
1795	Marries Anna Symmes
1798	Appointed secretary of the Northwest Territory
1799	Elected delegate to the U.S. House of Representatives
1800	Appointed governor of the Indiana Territory
1811	Leads white American forces in the Battle of Tippecanoe
1812	Receives commission as general; resigns as governor
1813	Battle of the Thames
1814	Resigns from the army

1816–19	Serves as a member of the U.S. House of Representatives
1819–21	Serves as an Ohio state senator
1825	Elected to the U.S. Senate
1828	Appointed U.S. envoy to Colombia
1829	Returns to Ohio to pursue private business ventures
1831	Runs unsuccessfully for the U.S. Senate
1836–40	Serves as county court clerk in Cincinnati
1836	Runs for president as a sectional Whig candidate
1840	Elected president on the Whig ticket
1841	Sworn in on March 4; dies in office on April 4

Selected Bibliography

BOOKS

Anthony, Carl Sferrazza. *First Ladies*. New York: Quill, 1990.

Barnes, Thurlow Weed. *Life of Thurlow Weed*. Boston: Houghton Mifflin, 1884.

Brodie, Fawn. *Thaddeus Stevens, Scourge of the South*. New York: Norton, 1966.

Cleaves, Freeman. *Old Tippecanoe*. Newtown, Conn.: American Political Biography Press, 1990.

Collins, Gail. *Scorpion Tongues: Gossip, Celebrity, and American Politics*. New York: Harcourt Brace, 1999.

Goebel, Dorothy Burne. *William Henry Harrison*. Indianapolis: Historical Bureau of the Indiana Library and Historical Department, 1926.

Green, James. *William Henry Harrison, His Life and Times*. Richmond, Va.: Garret and Massie, 1941.

Gunderson, Robert Gray. *The Log-Cabin Campaign*. Westport, Conn.: Greenwood Press, 1977.

Heidler, David, and Jeanne Heidler. *Henry Clay: The Essential American*. New York: Random House, 2010.

Holt, Michael F. *The Rise and Fall of the American Whig Party*. New York: Oxford University Press, 1999.

Howe, Daniel Walker. *What Hath God Wrought.* New York: Oxford University Press, 2007.

Janken, Kenneth Robert. *White.* New York: The New Press, 2003.

Larkin, Jack. *The Reshaping of Everyday Life.* New York: Harper-Perennial, 1989.

May, Gary. *John Tyler.* New York: Times Books, 2008.

Moore, Anne Chieko. *Benjamin Harrison: Centennial President.* Hauppauge, N.Y.: Nova Science, 2009.

Norton, Anthony Banning. *The Great Revolution of 1840.* Mount Vernon, Ohio: A. B. Norton, 1888.

Owens, Robert. *Mr. Jefferson's Hammer: William Henry Harrison and the Origins of American Indian Policy.* Norman: University of Oklahoma Press, 2007.

Peterson, Norma. *The Presidencies of William Henry Harrison and John Tyler.* Lawrence: University of Kansas Press, 1989.

Schlesinger, Arthur M., Jr. *History of American Presidential Elections, 1789–1986.* Vol. 1. New York: Chelsea House Publishers, 1985.

Sugden, John. *Blue Jacket: Warrior of the Shawnees.* Lincoln: University of Nebraska Press, 2000.

———. *Tecumseh: A Life.* New York: Henry Holt, 1998.

Weeks, Stephen. *Southern Quakers and Slavery: A Study in Institutional History.* Baltimore: Johns Hopkins Press, 1896.

Widmer, Ted. *Martin Van Buren.* New York: Times Books, 2005.

Wilentz, Sean. *Andrew Jackson.* New York: Times Books, 2005.

Woodward, C. Vann. *Mary Chesnut's Civil War.* New Haven, Conn.: Yale University Press, 1981.

PERIODICALS

Battin, Richard. "Mad Anthony Wayne at Fallen Timbers." *Early American Review,* Fall 1996.

Elliston, George. "Old Harrison House, Now Forlorn, May Become a Shrine." *Cincinnati Times-Star,* May 7, 1940.

Acknowledgments

A while back I got a letter from a woman who said she was a great fan of the Times Books series on the American presidents and that she had just completed the life of Martin Van Buren. "So what I want to know," she continued, "is—*where is William Henry Harrison???*"

I would like to thank that correspondent, whose name I've forgotten, for giving me the incentive to finish this book.

Also, all my family in Cincinnati, who were extremely supportive when I kept bringing up William Henry during holiday celebrations.

Thanks to all the great people at Henry Holt and Company who worked on the project, particularly Paul Golob, who was a wonderful editor and always laughed at my Harrison anecdotes. Sean Wilentz was extremely kind when he checked out my work. I also want to acknowledge the late Arthur Schlesinger, Jr., who was overseeing the project when I began, and who sent me a very encouraging letter in which he said that writing a biography of a president because your father tore down his house was one of the better reasons he'd ever heard for getting into this kind of undertaking.

Whenever I write anything, I have to express my appreciation to my amazing agent, Alice Martell.

And say that without my husband, Dan Collins, none of it would be any fun.

Index

ABOUT THE AUTHOR

GAIL COLLINS is an op-ed columnist for *The New York Times*, where she previously served as editorial page editor—the first woman to hold that position. She is the author of *When Everything Changed: The Amazing Journey of American Women from 1960 to the Present*; *America's Women: 400 Years of Dolls, Drudges, Helpmates, and Heroines*; and *Scorpion Tongues: Gossip, Celebrity, and American Politics*. She lives in New York City with her husband, Dan Collins.